SING
WITH THE BAND

30 POPULAR SONGS FOR FEMALE SINGERS

ISBN 978-1-61774-050-3

CORPORATION
7777 W. BLUEMOUND RD. P.O. BOX 13819 MILWAUKEE, WI 53213

Visit Hal Leonard Online at
www.halleonard.com

VOCAL WARM-UP EXERCISES

TRACK 1

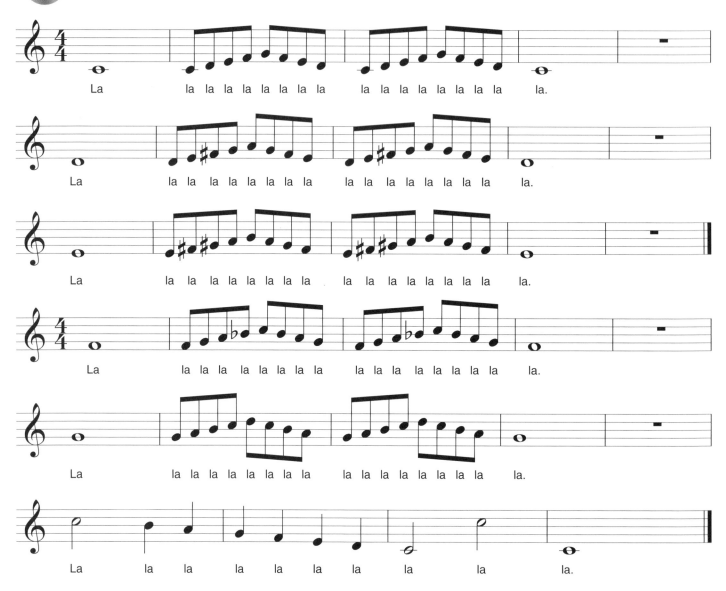

Mid-Continent Public Library
15616 East Highway 24
Independence, MO 64050

CD #1

CD #2

Alone

Words and Music by Billy Steinberg and Tom Kelly

Intro
Slowly

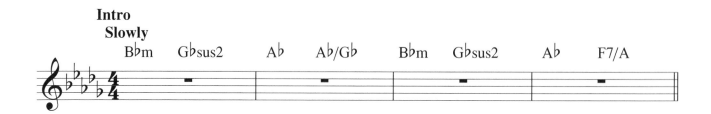

Verse

Female:

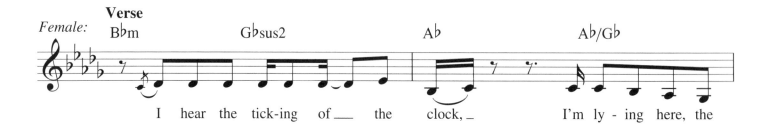

I hear the tick-ing of ___ the clock, ___ I'm ly-ing here, the

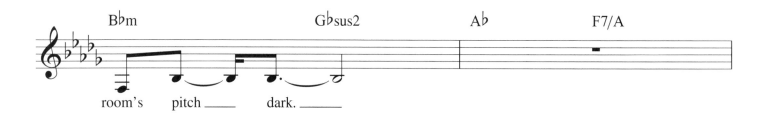

room's pitch ___ dark. ___

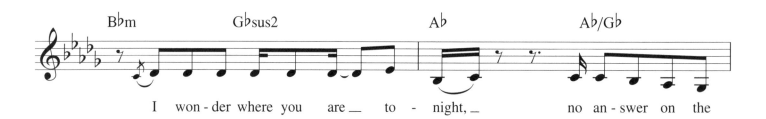

I won-der where you are ___ to-night, ___ no an-swer on the

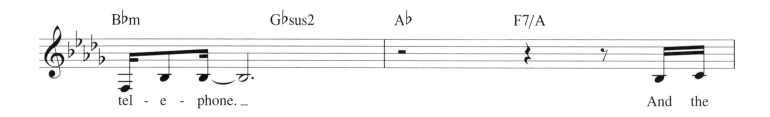

tel-e-phone. ___ And the

night goes by so ___ ver-y slow, oh. ___ I

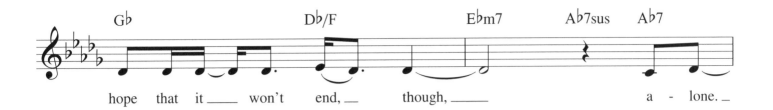

hope that it ___ won't end, ___ though, _____ a - lone. ___

℅ Chorus

___ 'Til now, ___ I

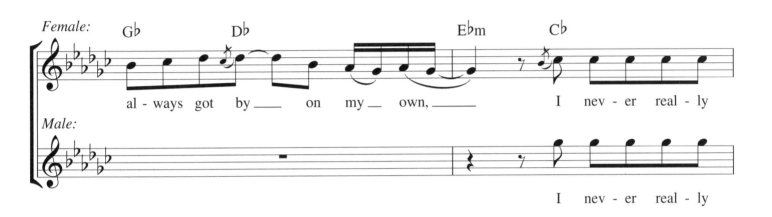

Female:

al - ways got by ___ on my ___ own, _____ I nev - er real - ly

Male:

I nev - er real - ly

cared un - til I met you. And now it

cared un - til I met you. And now it

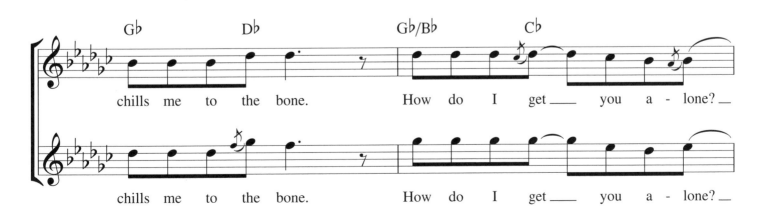

chills me to the bone. How do I get ___ you a - lone? ___

chills me to the bone. How do I get ___ you a - lone? ___

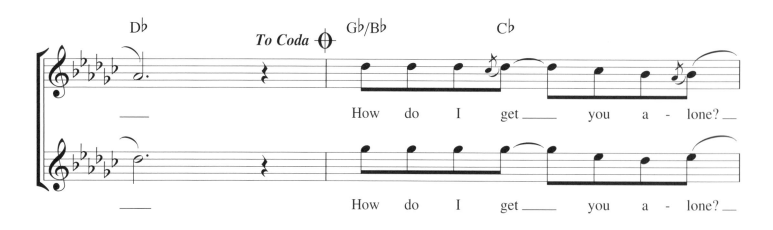

To Coda

How do I get ___ you a - lone? ___

How do I get ___ you a - lone? ___

Verse

Male:

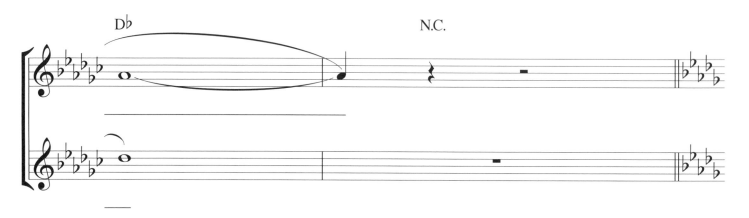

You don't know how long I have want - ed to touch your lips and

hold you tight, ___ yeah. ___

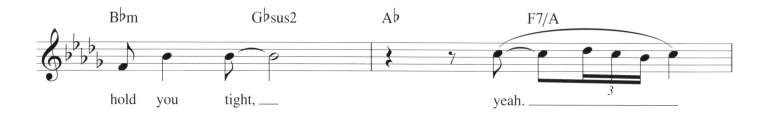

Female:

You don't know how long I have wait - ed, and I was gon - na

Male:

You don't know how long I have wait - ed, and I was gon - na

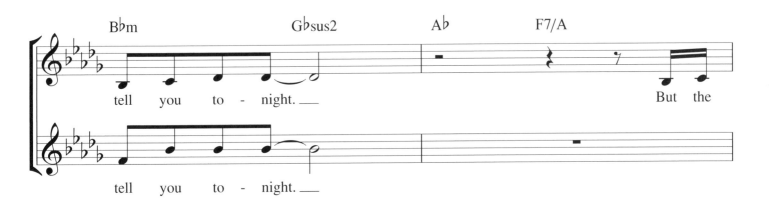

tell you to - night. ___

tell you to - night. ___

But the

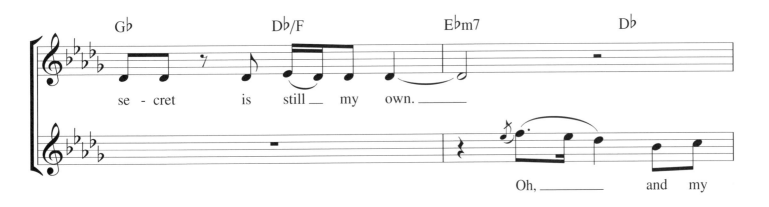

se - cret is still ___ my own. ___

Oh, ___ and my

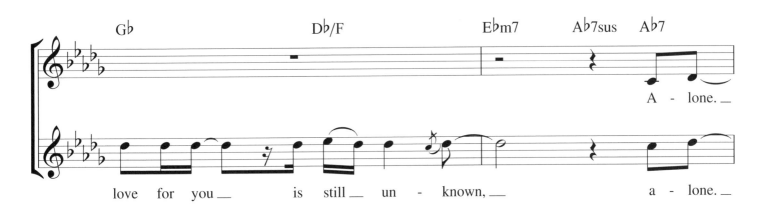

love for you ___ is still ___ un - known, ___ a - lone. ___

A - lone. ___

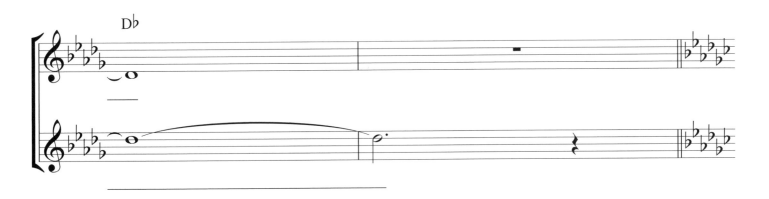

Pre-Chorus

Female: Ebm Cb Gb Db

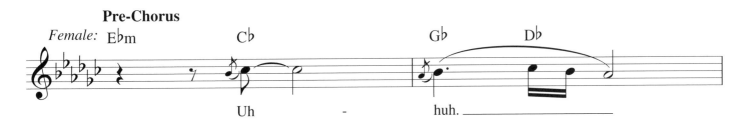

Uh - huh. ___

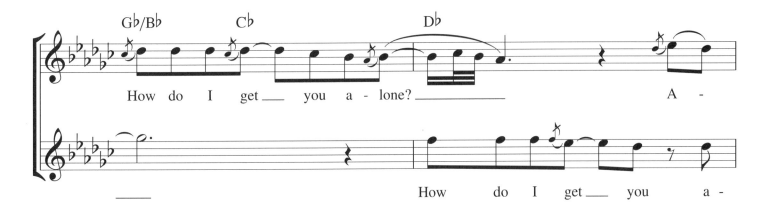

How do I get ___ you a - lone? ___

A -

___

How do I get ___ you a -

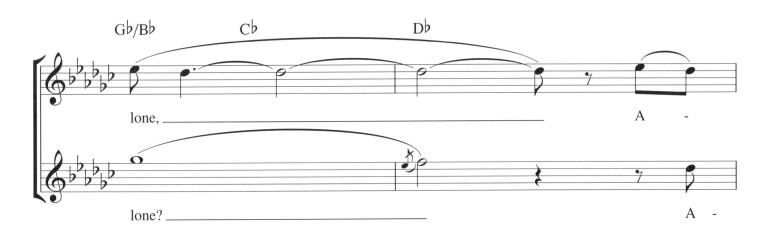

lone, ___

A -

lone? ___

A -

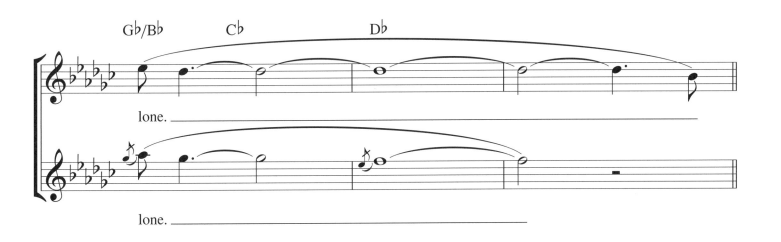

lone. ___

lone. ___

Outro

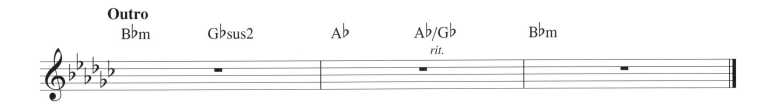

B♭m   G♭sus2   A♭   A♭/G♭   B♭m

rit.

Beautiful

Words and Music by Linda Perry

Crazy

Words and Music by Willie Nelson

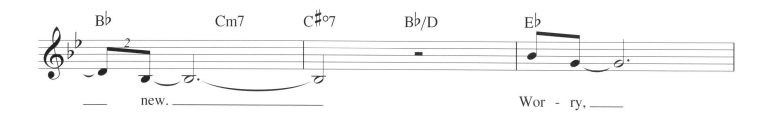

new. Wor - ry, ____

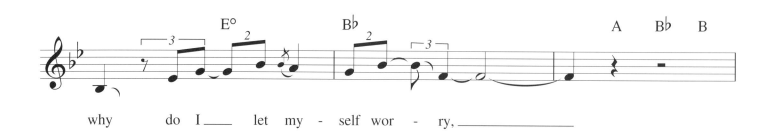

why do I ____ let my - self wor - ry, _____

won - d'rin' ___ what in the world ____ did I do? _____

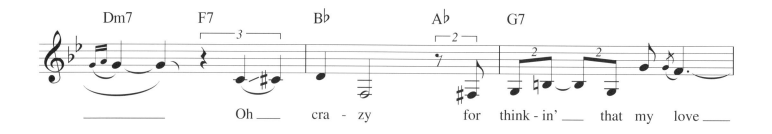

_____ Oh ____ cra - zy for think - in' ____ that my love ____

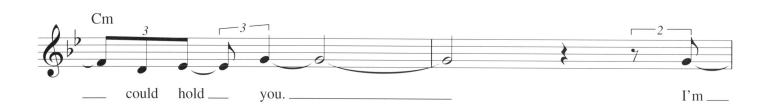

____ could hold ____ you. _____ I'm ____

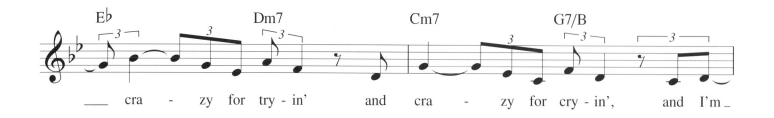

____ cra - zy for try - in' and cra - zy for cry - in', and I'm_

cra - zy for lov - in' you.

Verse

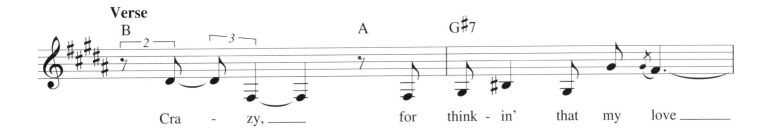

Cra - zy, for think - in' that my love

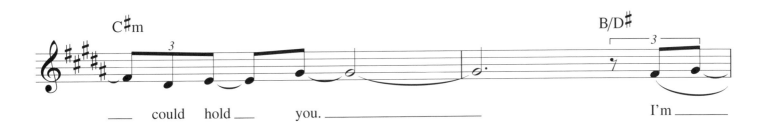

could hold you. I'm

cra - zy for try - in' and I'm cra - zy for cry - in', and I'm

cra - zy for lov - in' you.

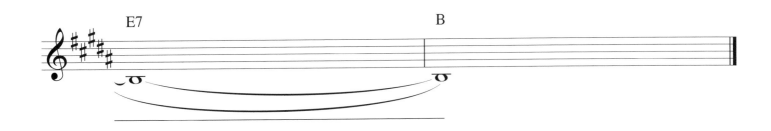

Before He Cheats

Words and Music by Josh Kear and Chris Tompkins

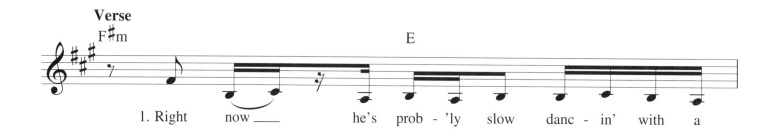

Verse

1. Right now ___ he's prob - 'ly slow danc - in' with a

bleach blonde tramp, and she's prob - 'ly get - tin' frisk - y.

A - right now ___ he's prob - 'ly buy - in' her some

fruit - y lit - tle drink, 'cause she can't ___ shoot whis - key.

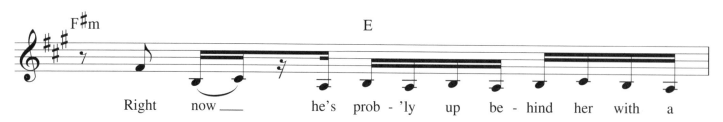

Right now ___ he's prob - 'ly up be - hind her with a

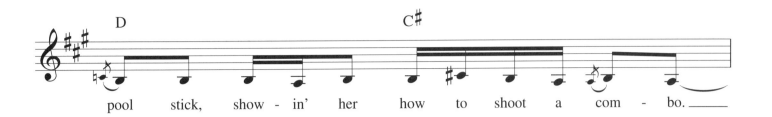

pool stick, show - in' her how to shoot a com - bo. _____

_____ And he don't know _____ I

Chorus

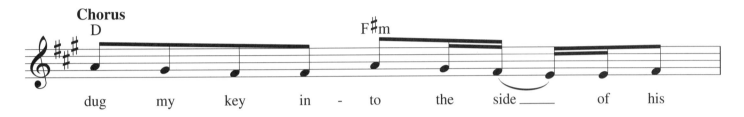

dug my key in - to the side _____ of his

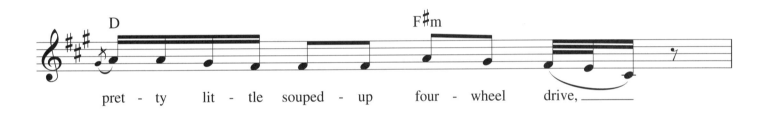

pret - ty lit - tle souped - up four - wheel drive, _____

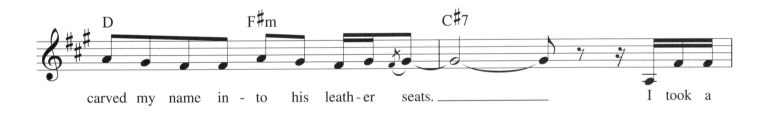

carved my name in - to his leath - er seats. _____ I took a

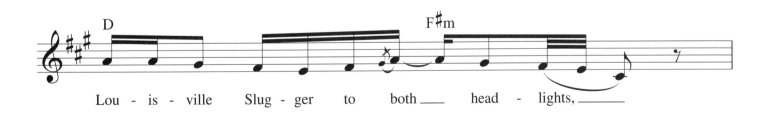

Lou - is - ville Slug - ger to both _____ head - lights, _____

slashed a hole _____ in all _____ four tires.

May - be next time ____ he'll think ____ be - fore ____ he ____

____ cheats. ____

Verse

2. Right now ____ she's prob - 'ly up sing - in' some ____

white trash ver - sion of Sha - ni - a kar - a - o - ke.

Right ____ now ____ she's prob - 'ly say - in', "I'm drunk,"

and he's a - think - in' that he's gon - na get ____ luck - y.

Right ____ now ____ he's prob - 'ly dab - bin' on three

dol - lars' worth ____ of that bath - room Po - lo. ____

Oh, and he don't know, _____ oh, _____ that I

Chorus

dug my key in - to the side _____ of his

pret - ty lit - tle souped - up four - wheel drive, _____

carved my _ name in - to his leath - er seats. _____ I took a

Lou - is - ville Slug - ger to both _ head - lights, _____

slashed a hole _____ in all _____ four tires, _____ and

may - be next time _____ he'll think _____ be - fore _____ he

_____ cheats. _____

Bridge

I might - 've saved a lit - tle trou - ble for the

next girl, _____ 'cause the next time that he cheats, _____

oh, ___ you know _ it won't be on ___ me, _____

no, _____ not on ____ me. _____

Chorus-Outro

'Cause I dug my key in - to the side _ of his

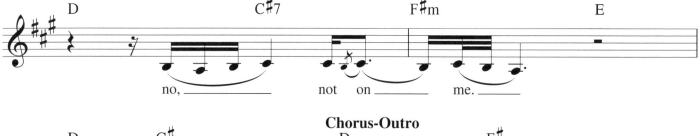

pret - ty lit - tle souped - up four - wheel drive, _____

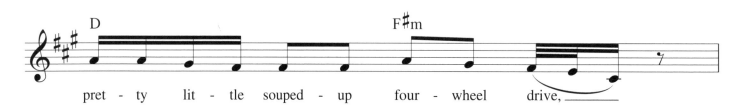

carved my _ name in - to his leath - er seats. _____ I took a

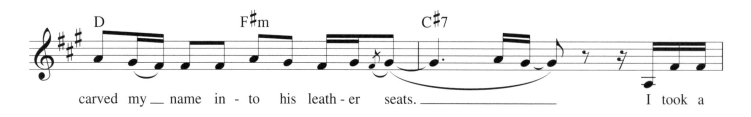

Lou - is - ville Slug - ger to both ___ head - lights, _____

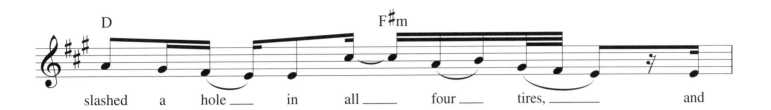

slashed a hole ___ in all ___ four ___ tires, _____ and

may - be next time ___ he'll think ___ be - fore ___ he ___

___ cheats, _____ oh, ___

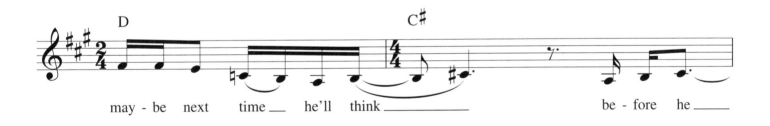

may - be next time ___ he'll think _____ be - fore he ___

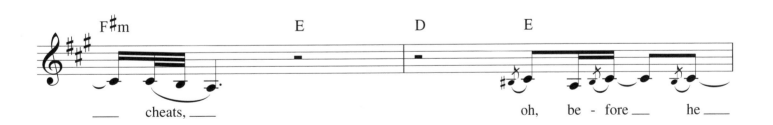

___ cheats, ___ oh, be - fore ___ he ___

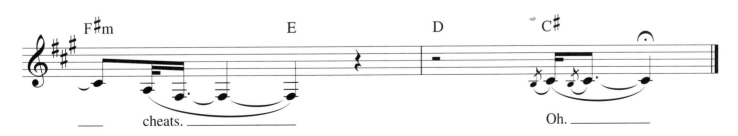

___ cheats. ___ Oh. ___

Big Girls Don't Cry

Words and Music by Stacy Ferguson and Toby Gad

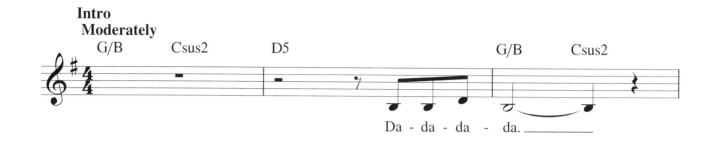

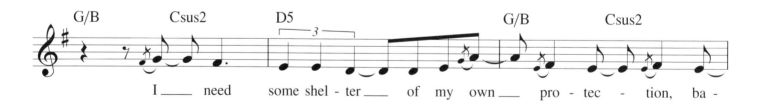

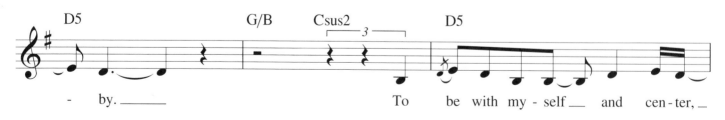

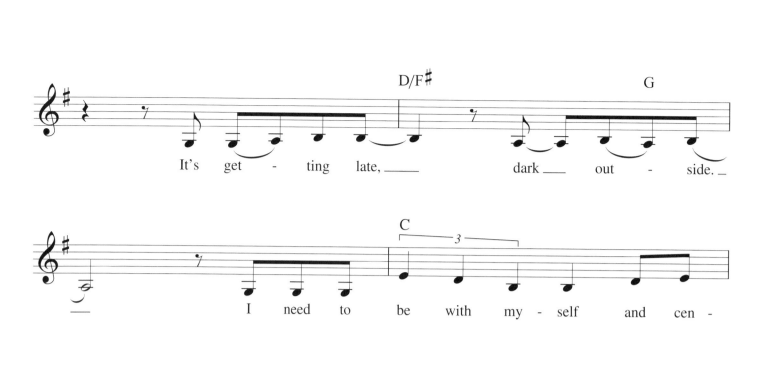

It's get - ting late, _____ dark ___ out - side. _

I need to be with my - self and cen -

ter, clar - i - ty, peace, ser - en - i - ty, _____ yeah. _____

Chorus

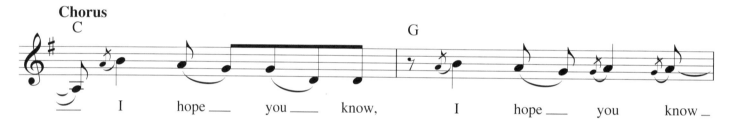

I hope ___ you ___ know, I hope ___ you know _

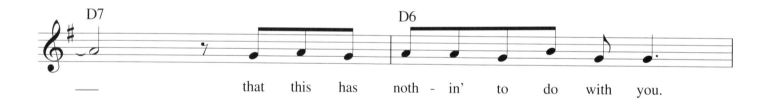

___ that this has noth - in' to do with you.

It's per - son - al. My - self ___ and I, ___

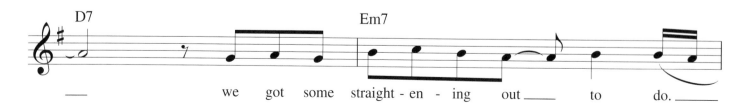

___ we got some straight - en - ing out ___ to do. _____

And I'm gon - na miss you — like a child miss - es their

blan - ket, — but I've got — to get a move — on — with my life. ____

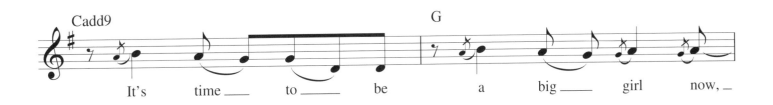

It's time ____ to ____ be a big ____ girl now, —

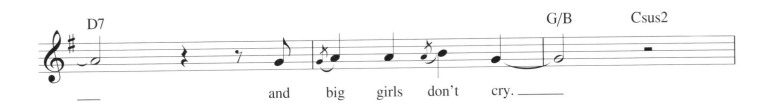

____ and big girls don't cry. _____

Don't _ cry, _____ don't cry, — don't _ cry.

Da - da - da - da - da - da. _____

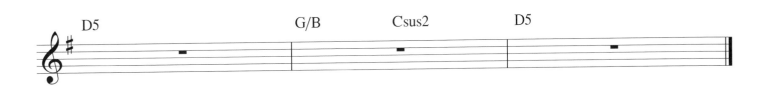

Breathe

Words and Music by Holly Lamar and Stephanie Bentley

Intro
Moderately fast

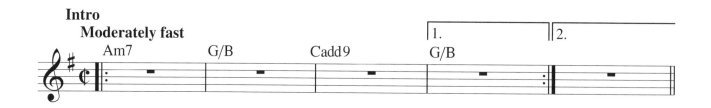

Verse

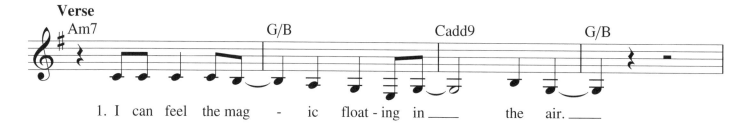

1. I can feel the mag - ic float-ing in ___ the air. ___

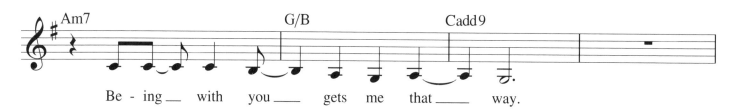

Be - ing ___ with you ___ gets me that ___ way.

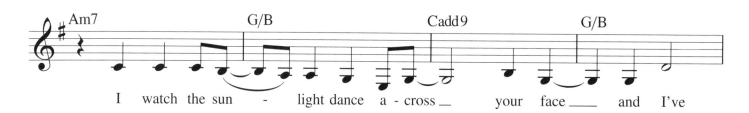

I watch the sun - light dance a - cross ___ your face ___ and I've

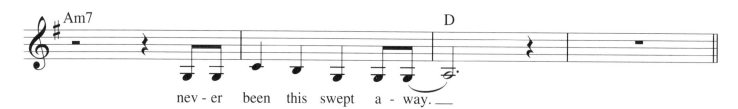

nev - er been this swept a - way. ___

Verse

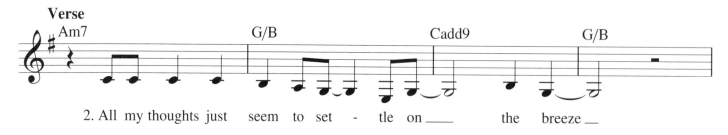

2. All my thoughts just seem to set - tle on ___ the breeze ___

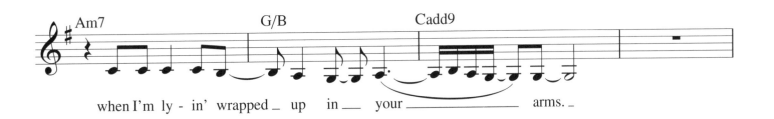

when I'm ly - in' wrapped __ up in __ your _____ arms. __

The whole world just fades a - way, __ and the on - ly thing I _____

hear is the beat - ing of __ your heart. _____ 'Cause I can feel you

𝄋 Chorus

breathe, it's wash - ing o - ver me, and sud - den - ly I'm melt - ing in - to you. __

__ There's noth - ing left to prove, ba - by, all we need is just __ to be __

_____ caught __ up in the touch, the slow and stead - y

rush. Ba - by, is - n't that the way __ that love's __ sup - posed _____

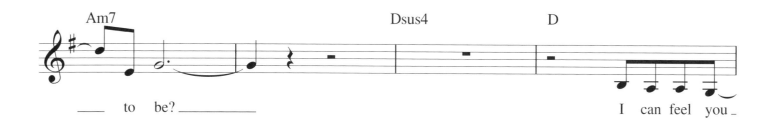

_____ to be? _____ I can feel you _____

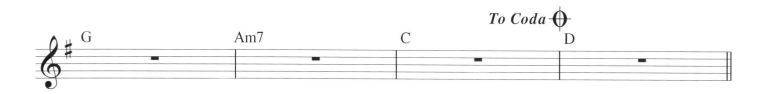

_____ breathe. _____ Just _____

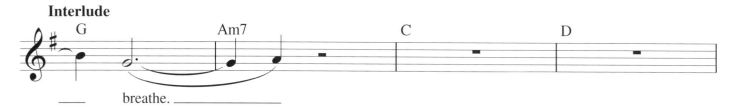

Interlude

_____ breathe. _____

Verse

3. In a way I know _ my heart _ is wak - ing up _____

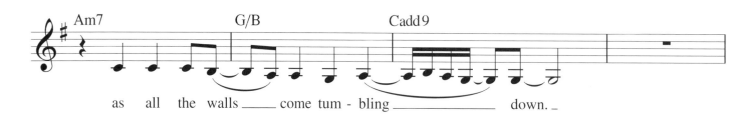

as all the walls _____ come tum - bling _____ down. _

Clos-er than I've ev - er felt _ be - fore, _ and I know _ and you _____

know   there's no   need   for   words _ right   now.   'Cause I   can feel you

Caught _ up in the   touch,   the slow and stead-y   rush.   Ba-by, is-n't

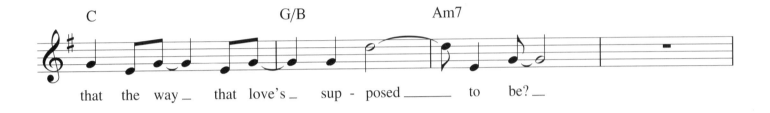

that   the   way _   that   love's _   sup-posed _____   to   be? _

I   can   feel   you ___   breathe. _____

Just _____   breathe.

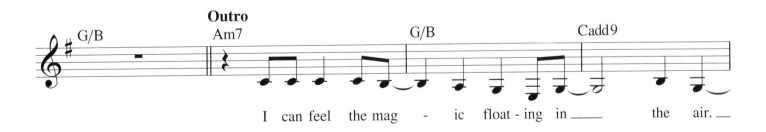

I   can   feel   the   mag   -   ic   float-ing   in _____   the   air. _

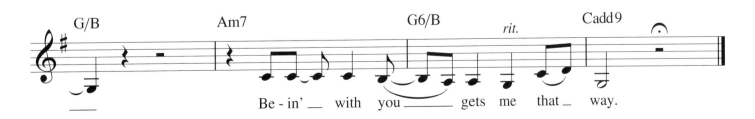

Be-in' _ with   you _____   gets   me   that _   way.

Dancing Queen

Words and Music by Benny Andersson, Björn Ulvaeus and Stig Anderson

Intro-Chorus
Moderately

You can dance, _ you can jive, _____ hav - ing _ the time of _ your

life. ___ Ooh, _____ see that _ girl, _ watch that _ scene, _ dig- gin' the

danc - ing _ queen. _____

Verse

1. Fri-day night _ and the lights are low, ___

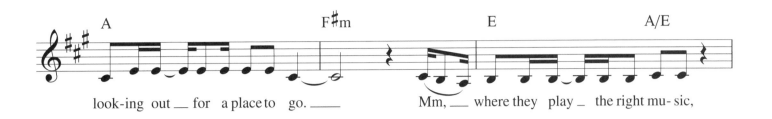

look-ing out __ for a place to go. __ Mm, __ where they play __ the right mu- sic,

get-ting in __ the swing, __ you come to look for a king. __

Verse

2. An - y - bod - y could be that guy, __

night is young __ and the mu - sic's high; __

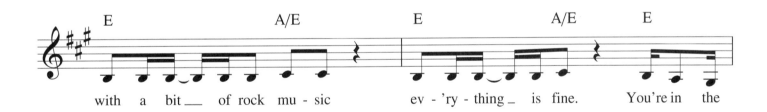

with a bit __ of rock mu - sic ev - 'ry - thing __ is fine. You're in the

mood for a dance, __ and when __ you get the __ chance... __

Chorus

__ You are __ the danc - ing __ queen, __ young and __ sweet, __ on - ly

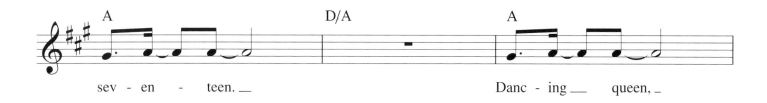

sev - en - teen. ___   Danc - ing ___ queen, ___

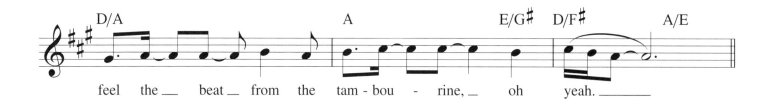

feel the ___ beat ___ from the tam - bou - rine, ___ oh yeah. _____

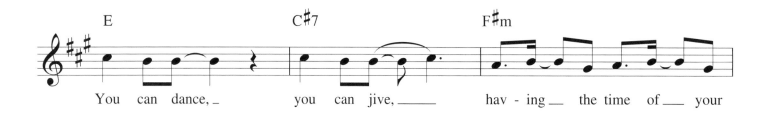

You can dance, _   you can jive, _____   hav - ing ___ the time of ___ your

life. ___ Ooh, _____ see that ___ girl, _ watch that ___ scene, _ dig- gin' the

To Coda ⊕

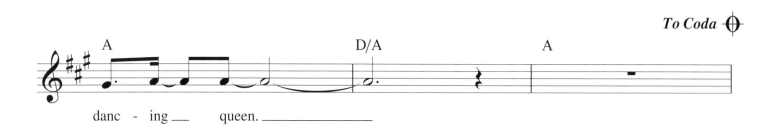

danc - ing ___ queen. _____

Verse

3. You're a teas - er, you turn 'em on, _____

leave them burn - ing and then you're gone;

look - ing out __ for an - oth - er, an - y - one __ will do. You're in the

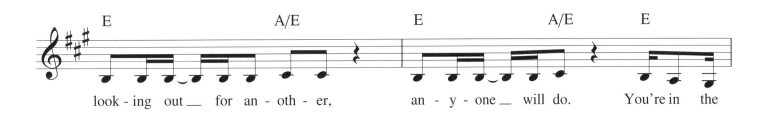

mood for a dance, __ and when you get the __ chance... _____

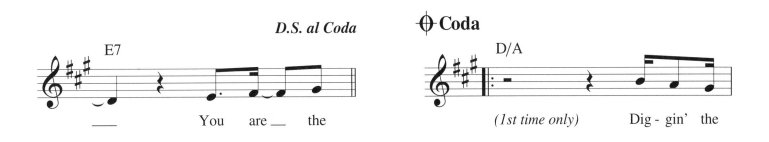

D.S. al Coda   𝄋 **Coda**

___ You are __ the   *(1st time only)*   Dig - gin' the

Repeat and fade

danc - ing ___ queen. _____

Don't Know Why

Words and Music by Jesse Harris

Intro
Moderately slow

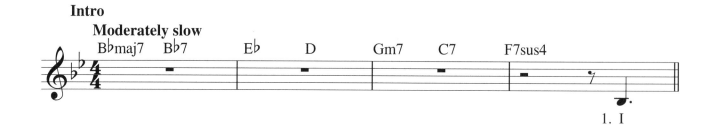

1. I

Verse

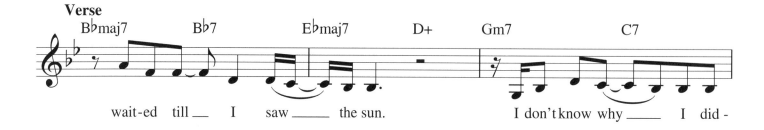

wait-ed till __ I saw ____ the sun. I don't know why ____ I did -

n't come. __ I left you by _____ the house _ of fun. __

I don't know why ____ I did - n't come, __ I don't know why I did-n't _

__ come. When I saw _____ the break _ of day,

I wished that I _____ could fly ___ a-way 'stead of kneel - ing in

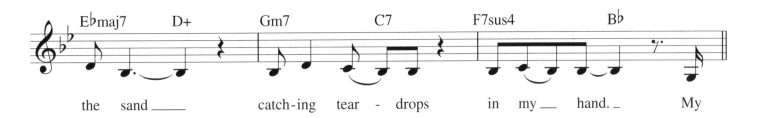

the sand _____ catch-ing tear - drops in my _ hand. _ My

Bridge

heart is _ drenched _ in _____ wine, _ but

you'll be _ on _____ my _____ mind _ for - ev - er. _

Verse

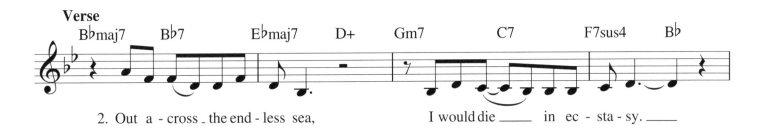

2. Out a - cross _ the end - less sea, I would die _____ in ec - sta - sy. _____

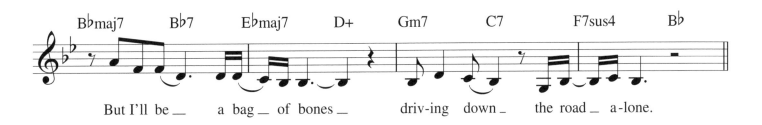

But I'll be _ a bag _ of bones _ driv-ing down _ the road _ a-lone.

Bridge

My heart _ is drenched _ in _____ wine, _ but

you'll be _ on _____ my _____ mind _ for - ev - er. _

Piano Solo

Outro-Verse

Some thing has __ to make __ you run.   I don't know why ____ I did-

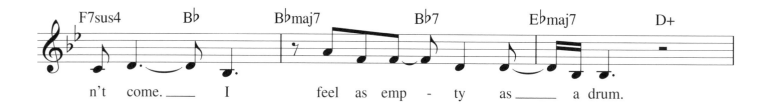

n't come. ____ I   feel as emp - ty as ____ a drum.

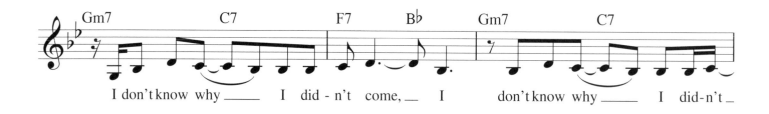

I don't know why ____ I did - n't come, __ I   don't know why ____ I did-n't __

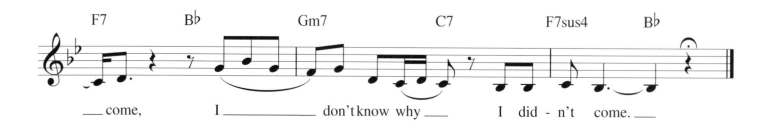

__ come,   I ____ don't know why __   I did - n't come. __

Dreams

Words and Music by Stevie Nicks

Chorus

40

Outro-Chorus

43

From a Distance

Words and Music by Julie Gold

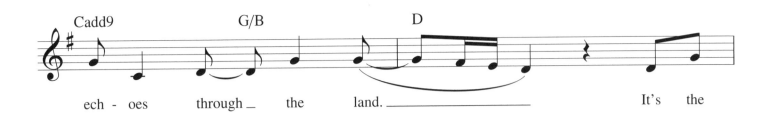

ech - oes   through __ the   land. _____   It's the

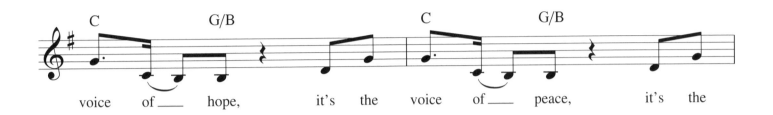

voice   of ___ hope,   it's the   voice   of ___ peace,   it's the

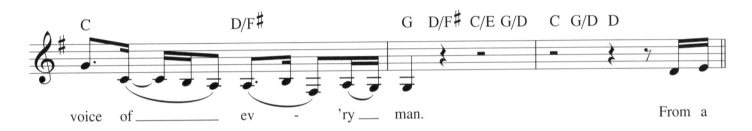

voice   of _____ ev - 'ry __ man.   From a

Verse

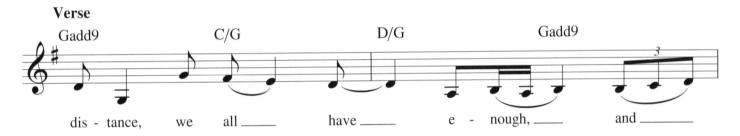

dis - tance,   we   all ___   have ___   e - nough, ___   and _____

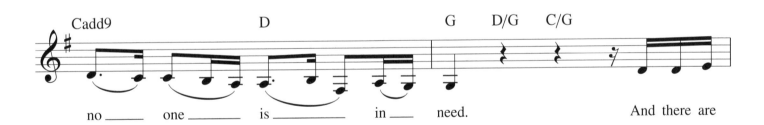

no ___ one ___ is ___ in ___ need.   And there are

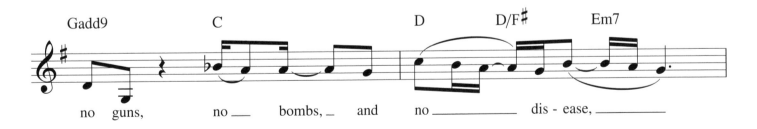

no   guns,   no __ bombs, __ and   no _____ dis - ease, _____

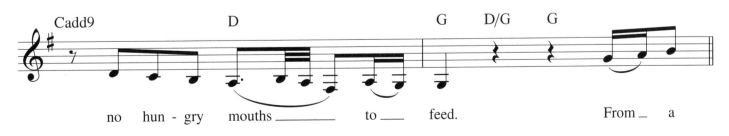

no   hun - gry   mouths _____ to __ feed.   From _ a

Chorus

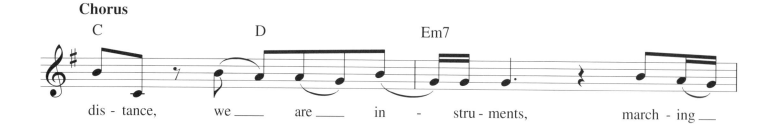

dis - tance, we ___ are ___ in - stru - ments, march - ing ___

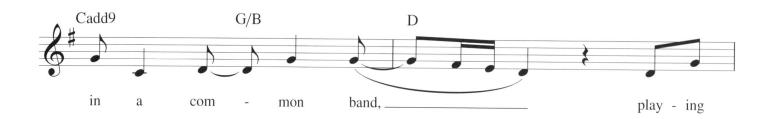

in a com - mon band, _____ play - ing

songs of ___ hope, play - ing songs of ___ peace. They're the

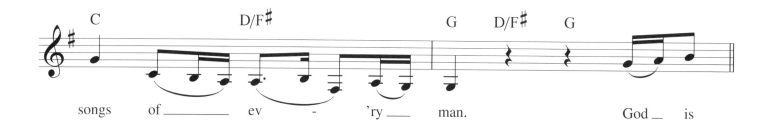

songs of _____ ev - 'ry ___ man. God ___ is

watch - ing us, ___ God ___ is watch - ing us, ___ God ___ is

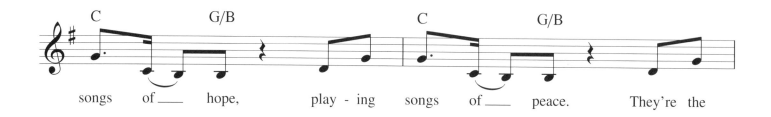

watch - ing us from a dis - tance. ___

From a

Verse

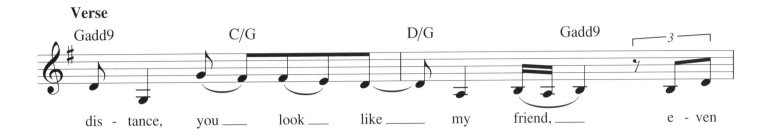

dis - tance, you ___ look ___ like ___ my friend, ___ e - ven

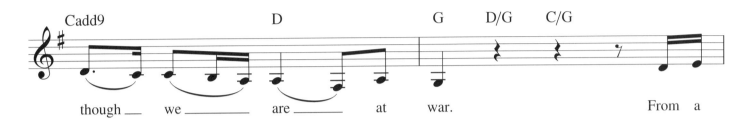

though ___ we ___ are ___ at war. From a

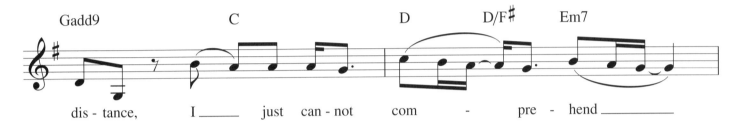

dis - tance, I ___ just can - not com - pre - hend ___

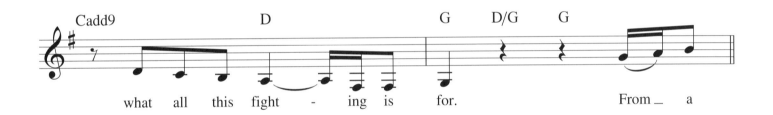

what all this fight - ing is for. From ___ a

Chorus

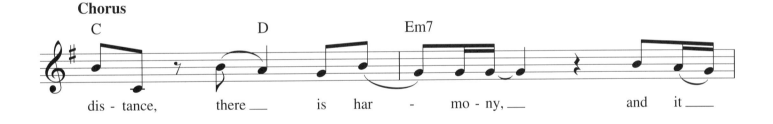

dis - tance, there ___ is har - mo - ny, ___ and it ___

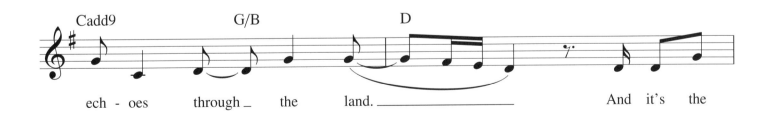

ech - oes through ___ the land. ___ And it's the

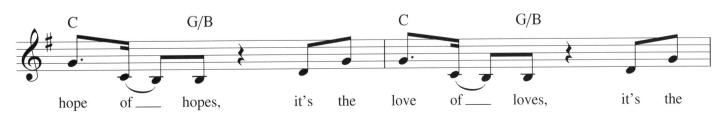

hope of ___ hopes, it's the love of ___ loves, it's the

heart _____ of ev - 'ry __ man. _____ It's the

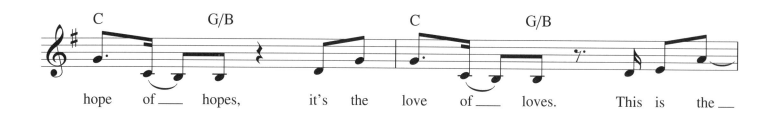

hope of __ hopes, it's the love of __ loves. This is the __

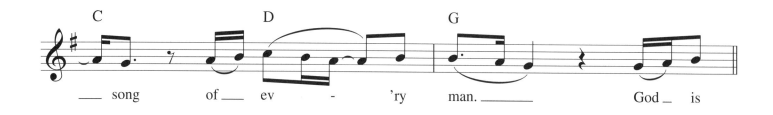

__ song of __ ev - 'ry man. _____ God _ is

watch - ing us, __ God _ is watch - ing _____ us, God _ is

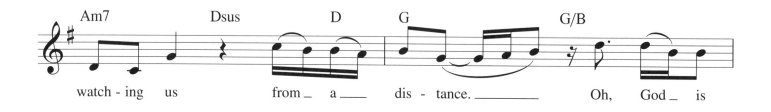

watch - ing us from _ a __ dis - tance. _____ Oh, God _ is

watch - ing us, __ God _ is watch - ing, _____ God _ is

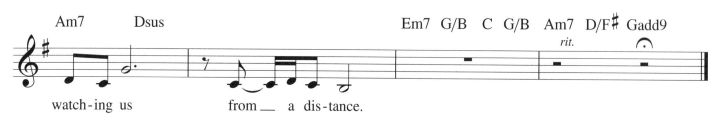

watch-ing us from _ a dis-tance.

Hot Stuff

Words and Music by Pete Bellotte, Harold Faltermeyer and Keith Forsey

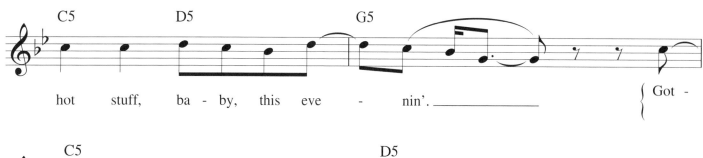

hot stuff, ba - by, this eve - nin'. _____ Got -

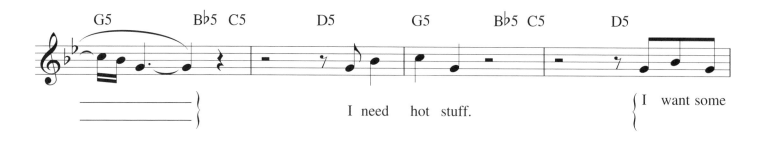

- ta have some hot stuff, got ___ to have some love ___ to - night. __
Got - ta have some lov - in', got ___ to have ___ love ___ to - night. __

_____ I need hot stuff. I want some

To Coda ⊕

hot love. I need hot stuff. _____
Hot love.

Interlude

D.S. al Coda

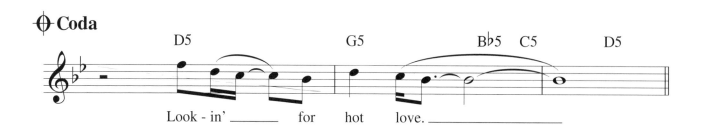

⊕ **Coda**

Look - in' ___ for hot love. _____

Guitar Solo

Interlude

Hot, hot, hot, hot stuff. _____ Hot, hot, hot.

Chorus

How's a - bout some hot stuff, ba - by, this eve -

- nin'? _____ I need some hot stuff, ba - by, to - night. _____ Look - in' for my

hot stuff, ba - by, this eve - nin'. _____ I need

some hot stuff, ba - by, to - night. Yeah, __ yeah. I want some

Outro

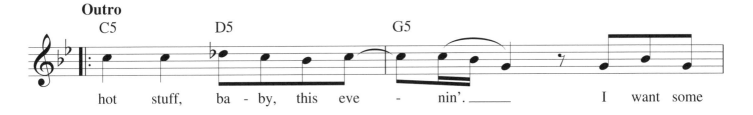

hot stuff, ba - by, this eve - nin'. _____ I want some

Repeat and fade

hot stuff, ba - by, to - night. Yeah, __ yeah, yeah, yeah. Some

Additional Lyrics

2. Lookin' for a lover who needs another,
   Don't want another night on my own.
   Want to share my love with a warm-blood lover,
   Want to bring a wild man back home.

I Feel the Earth Move

Words and Music by Carole King

Intro
Moderately

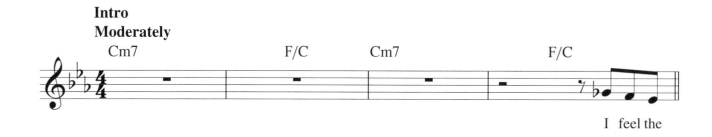

I feel the

Chorus

earth move un-der my feet. I feel the sky tum-bl-in' down. __

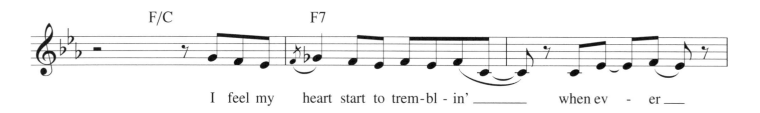

I feel my heart start to trem-bl-in' _____ when ev - er __

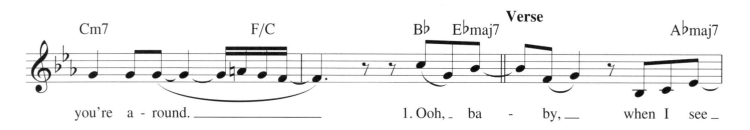

you're a - round. _____ 1. Ooh, _ ba - by, _ when I see _

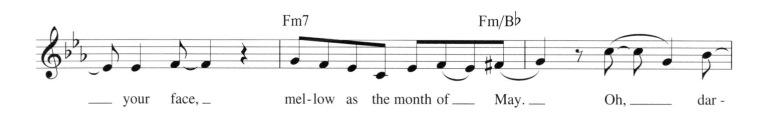

__ your face, _ mel-low as the month of __ May. _ Oh, _____ dar -

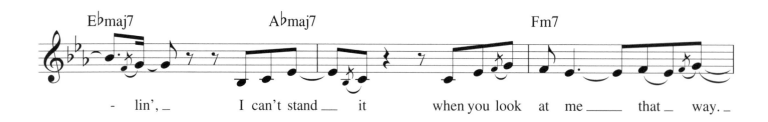

- lin', _ I can't stand __ it when you look at me ____ that _ way. _

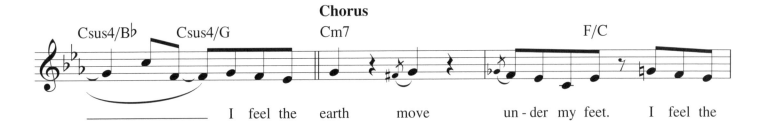

Chorus

Csus4/B♭ Csus4/G Cm7 F/C

_____ I feel the earth move un-der my feet. I feel the

Cm7 F/C F7

sky tum-bl-in' down. ___ I feel my heart start to trem-bl-in' ____

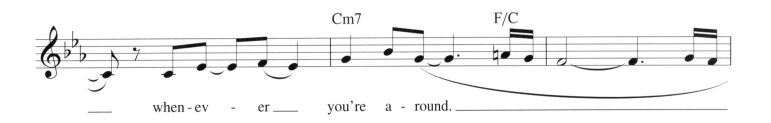

Cm7 F/C

___ when-ev - er ___ you're a - round. _____

Interlude

Cm7 F/C Cm7 **14**

_____

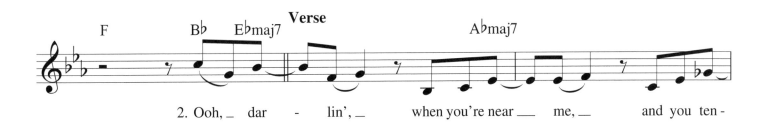

Verse

F B♭ E♭maj7 A♭maj7

2. Ooh, ___ dar - lin', ___ when you're near ___ me, ___ and you ten-

Fm7 A♭maj7/B♭ E♭maj7 A♭maj7

- der - ly call ___ my ___ name. ___ I _____ know ___ that ___ my e - mo-

- tions are some - thin' I ___ just ___ can't tame. ___ I just got to have you,

ba - by. ___ Ah, ah, ___ ah. Ah, ah, ___ ah, yeah. ___

Chorus

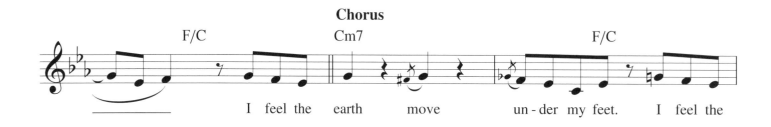

___ I feel the earth move un - der my feet. I feel the

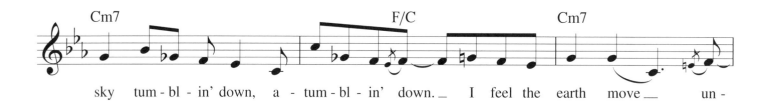

sky tum - bl - in' down, a - tum - bl - in' down. ___ I feel the earth move ___ un -

- der my feet. I feel the sky tum - bl - in' down, a - tum - bl - in' down. ___ I just a -

Bridge

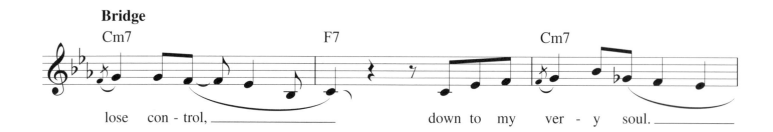

lose con - trol, ___ down to my ver - y soul. ___

I get a   hot and cold _____ all ___ o-

Chorus

- ver, all o - ver, all o - ver, all o - ver. I feel the   earth   move

un - der my feet.   I feel the   sky tum - bl - in' down, a - tum - bl - in' down. ___ I feel the

earth   move ___   un - der my feet.   I feel the   sky tum - bl - in' down, a -

rit.

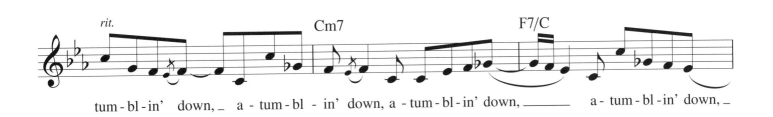

tum - bl - in' down, ___ a - tum - bl - in' down, a - tum - bl - in' down, _____ a - tum - bl - in' down, ___

Freely

___   tum - bl - in' ___   down. _____

I Hope You Dance

Words and Music by Tia Sillers and Mark D. Sanders

Intro
Moderately

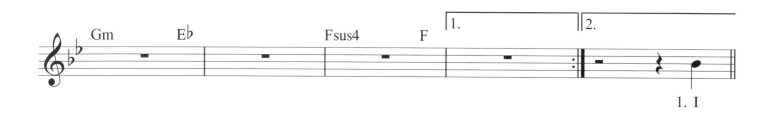

1. I

Verse

hope you nev-er lose ___ your sense of won - der. You get your

fill to eat, ___ but al - ways keep ___ that hun - ger. May you

nev-er take ___ one sin - gle breath ___ for grant - ed. ___ God for-bid ___

Verse

nev-er fear ____ those moun-tains in ___ the dis - tance. Nev-er

set - tle for _____ the path _____ of least _ re-sis - tence. Liv-in' might _

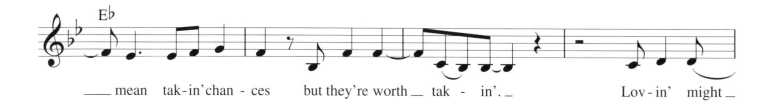

____ mean tak-in' chan - ces but they're worth __ tak - in'. _ Lov-in' might _

____ be a mis - take, but it's _ worth _____ mak - in'. 4. Don't

Verse

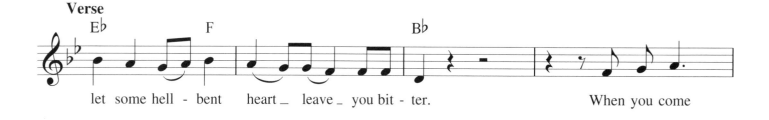

let some hell - bent heart _ leave _ you bit - ter. When you come

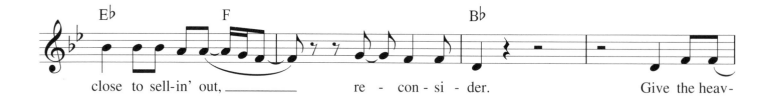

close to sell-in' out, _____ re - con - si - der. Give the heav-

- ens a-bove more ___ than just _ a pass - ing ___ glance. ___ And when you

get the choice to sit it out __ or __ dance, __ I hope __ you dance. __

Chorus

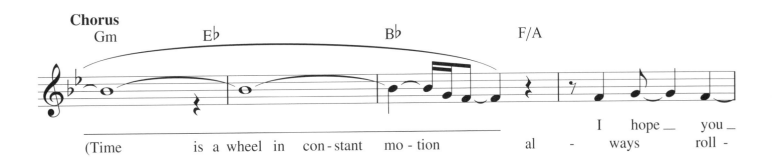

(Time is a wheel in con-stant mo-tion I hope __ you __ al - ways roll -

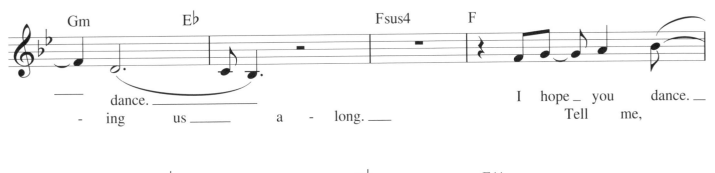

__ dance. __ I hope __ you dance. __
- ing us __ a - long. __ Tell me,

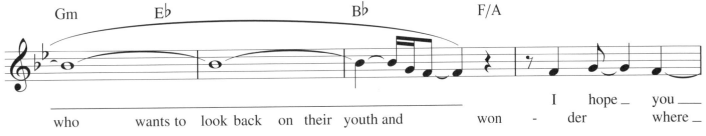

who wants to look back on their youth and I hope __ you __ won - der where __

D.S. al Coda

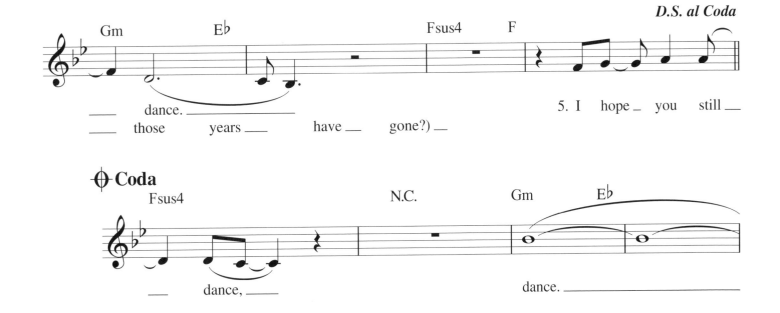

__ dance. __ 5. I hope __ you still __
__ those years __ have __ gone?) __

Coda

__ dance, __ dance. __

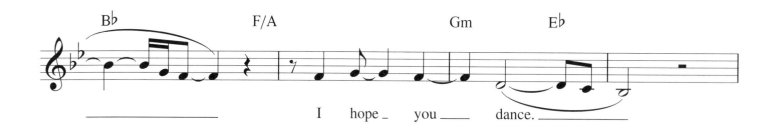

I hope _ you _ dance. _

Outro

I hope _ you dance. _

(Time is a wheel in con - stant

mo - tion al - ways roll - ing us _ a - long. _

I hope _ you _ dance. _

_ I hope _ you dance. _

Tell me, who wants to look back on their

youth and won - der where _ those years _

I hope _ you _ dance. _

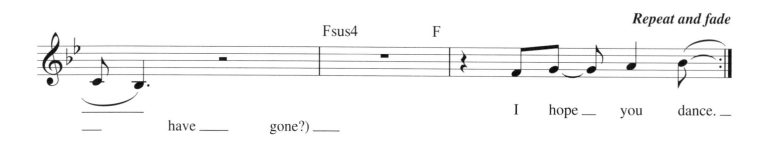

Repeat and fade

_ have _ gone?) _

I hope _ you dance. _

I Will Always Love You

Words and Music by Dolly Parton

Chorus

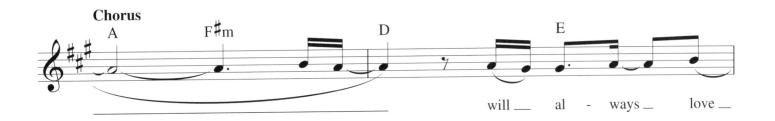

will al - ways love

you. I will al - ways love

Bridge

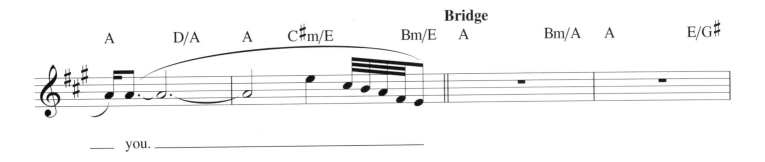

you.

Verse

3. I hope life treats you

kind, and I hope you have all you dreamed

of. _____ And I wish __ you joy ____ and __ hap - pi -

ness. _____ But a - bove all ____ this I ____ wish you ____ love. ____

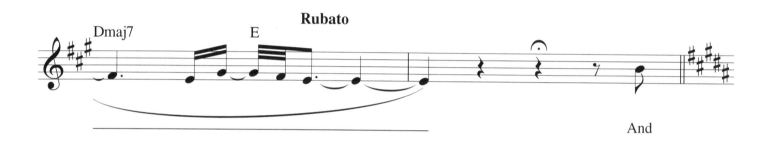

Rubato

And

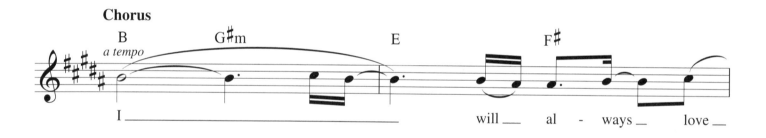

Chorus

a tempo

I _____ will ____ al - ways __ love ___

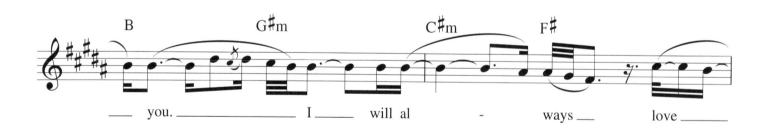

___ you. _____ I ____ will al - ways ___ love _____

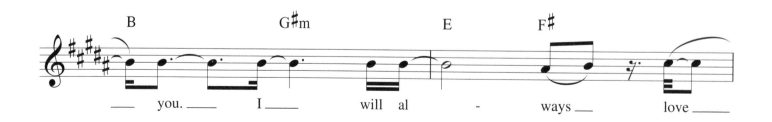

___ you. _____ I ____ will al - ways __ love _____

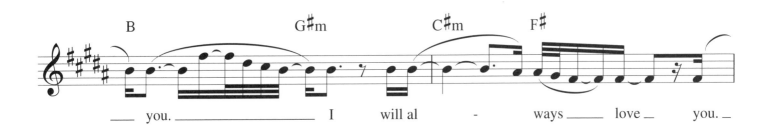

you. _____ I will al - ways _____ love _ you. _

I will _ al - ways love

you. _____ I will _ al - ways love _____

Rubato

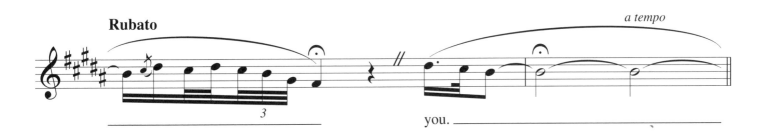

you. _____

Outro

Dar - ling I love _ you. _ Ooh, _____ I'll _

Rubato

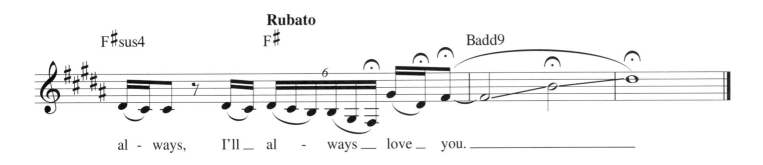

al - ways, I'll _ al - ways _ love _ you. _____

I Will Survive

Words and Music by Dino Fekaris and Frederick J. Perren

Intro-Verse
Freely

At first I was a-fraid, ___ I was pet-ri-fied. Kept think-in' I ___

___ could nev-er live ___ with-out ___ you by ___ my side. ___ But then I

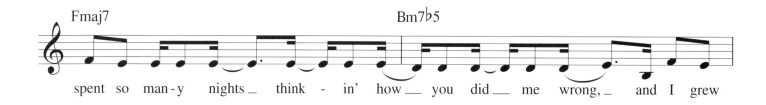

spent so man-y nights ___ think-in' how ___ you did ___ me wrong, ___ and I grew

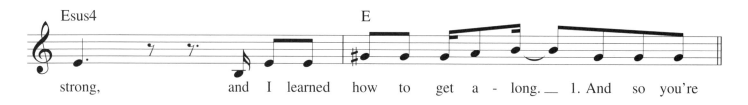

strong, and I learned how to get a-long. ___ 1. And so you're

Verse
Moderately

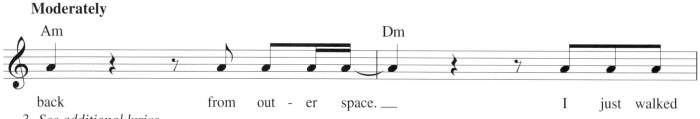

back from out-er space. ___ I just walked
3. *See additional lyrics*

in to find ___ you here ___ with that ___ sad look up-on ___ your face. I should-'ve changed ___

Additional Lyrics

3. And you see me, somebody new,
   I'm not that chained up little person
   Still in love with you.
   And so you felt like droppin' in
   And just expect me to be free.
   But now I'm savin' all my lovin'
   For someone who's lovin' me.

Love Story

Words and Music by Taylor Swift

Intro
Medium Country-Rock

Verse

We were both young when I first saw ___ you. I

close my eyes, ___ and the flash - back starts. ___ I'm stand - in'

there, on a bal - co - ny in sum - mer air.

I see the lights, ___ see the par - ty, the ball ___ gowns. I

Gadd9

see you make __ your way through the crowd, __ and say "Hel -

Bm7   Asus4

lo."   Lit - tle did I _____ know _____

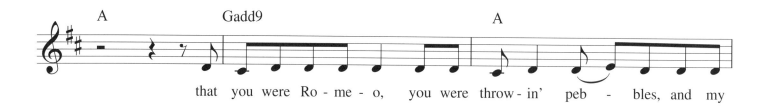

A   Gadd9   A

that you were Ro - me - o, you were throw - in' peb - bles, and my

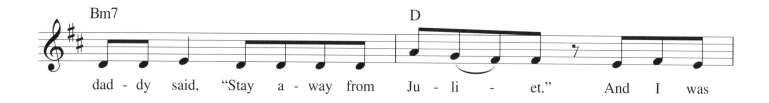

Bm7   D

dad - dy said, "Stay a - way from Ju - li - et." And I was

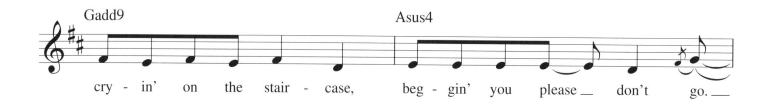

Gadd9   Asus4

cry - in' on the stair - case, beg - gin' you please __ don't go. __

Chorus

Bm7   Gadd9   A D

_____   And I __ said, "Ro - me - o take __ me

Gadd9   Asus4

some - where we can be a - lone. I'll be wait - ing.

Bm7

All that's left to do is run. You'll be the prince and

Gadd9

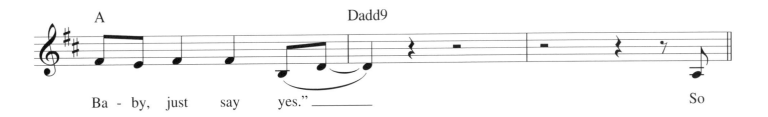

I'll be the prin - cess. It's a love sto - ry.

A   Dadd9

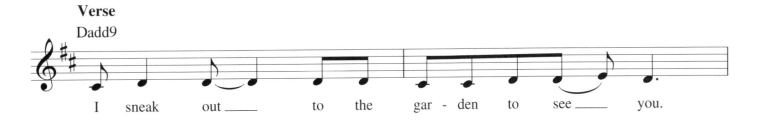

Ba - by, just say yes." _____ So

Verse

Dadd9

I sneak out _____ to the gar - den to see _____ you.

Gadd9

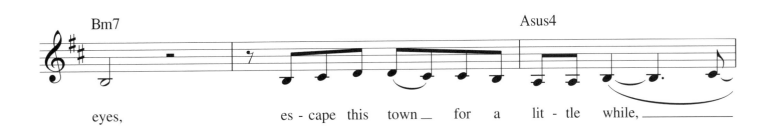

We keep qui - et, 'cause we're dead if they knew. ___ So close your

Bm7   Asus4

eyes, es - cape this town ___ for a lit - tle while, _____

A   Gadd9

__ oh, oh. ___ 'Cause you were Ro - me - o, I was the

71

scar - let let - ter, and my dad - dy said, "Stay a - way from

Ju - li - et." But you were ev - 'ry - thing to me, I was

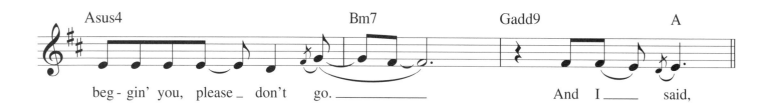

beg - gin' you, please _ don't go. _____ And I ____ said,

Chorus

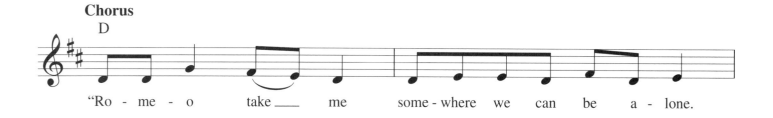

"Ro - me - o take ____ me some - where we can be a - lone.

I'll be wait - ing. All that's left to do is run.

You'll be the prince and I'll be the prin - cess.

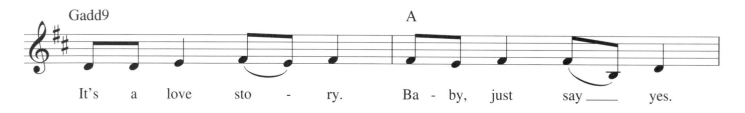

It's a love sto - ry. Ba - by, just say ____ yes.

Chorus

Ro - me - o, save ___ me. They're tryin' to tell me how to feel.

This love is dif - fi - cult, but it's real. _____

Don't be a - fraid, we'll make it out of this ___ mess.

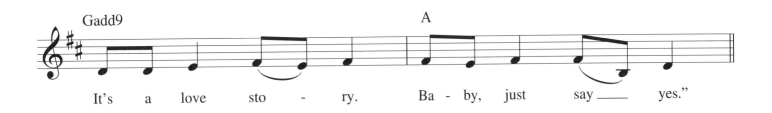

It's a love sto - ry. Ba - by, just say ___ yes."

Interlude

Oh, oh. _____

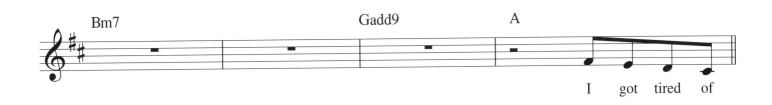

I got tired of

Bridge

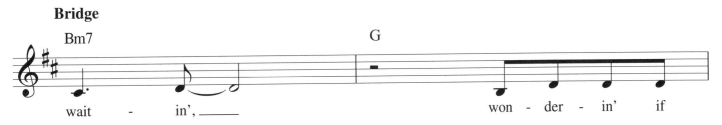

wait - in', _____ won - der - in' if

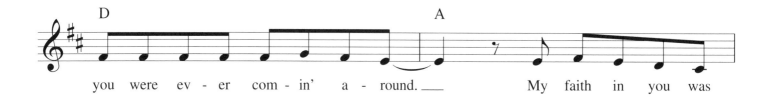

you were ev - er com - in' a - round. ___ My faith in you was

fad - in', when I met you on the out - skirts of

Chorus

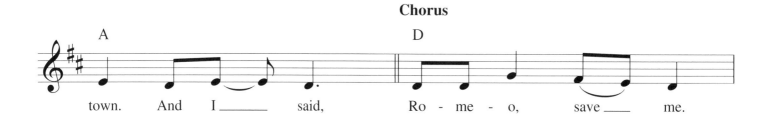

town. And I _____ said, Ro - me - o, save ___ me.

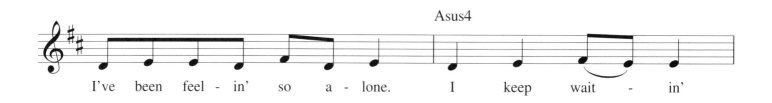

I've been feel - in' so a - lone. I keep wait - in'

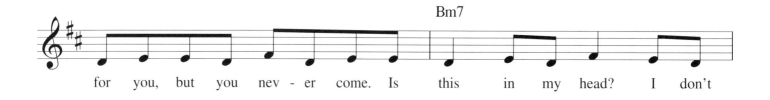

for you, but you nev - er come. Is this in my head? I don't

know what to think. He knelt to the ground and

Chorus

pulled out a ring and said: "Mar - ry me, Ju - li - et. You'll

Bsus4

nev - er have to be a - lone. I love you, ___ and

C#m7

that's all I real - ly know. I talked to your dad, go

Aadd9

pick out a white dress. It's a love sto - ry.

Outro

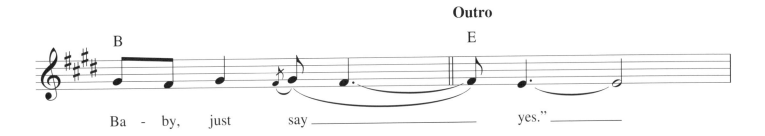

B   E

Ba - by, just say ___ yes." ___

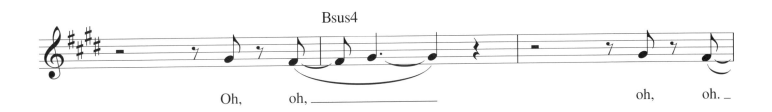

Bsus4

Oh, oh, ___ oh, oh. _

C#m7   Aadd9

'Cause we were both young when

N.C.

I first saw ___ you. ___

I'll Stand by You

Words and Music by Chrissie Hynde, Tom Kelly and Billy Steinberg

-fess   could make me love you ____ less. __   I'll stand by

Chorus

you,   I'll stand by ____ you. __   Won't let no-bod-y hurt __

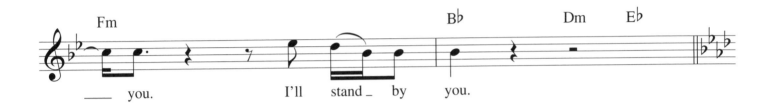

__ you.   I'll stand _ by you.

Verse

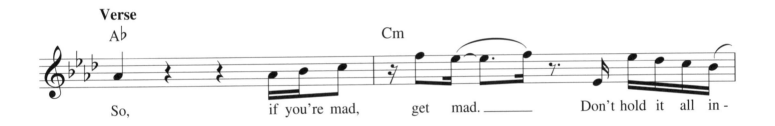

So,   if you're mad, get mad. _____ Don't hold it all in-

-side; __   come on and talk to me _____ now.

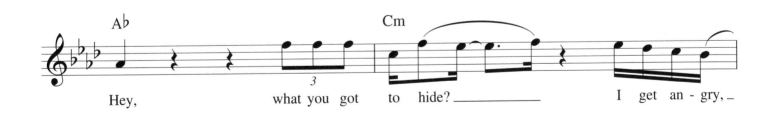

Hey,   what you got to hide? _____ I get an-gry, _

__ too.   Well, I'm a lot like you. ____ When you're _

Chorus

Outro

Keep Holding On

from the Twentieth Century Fox Motion Picture ERAGON
Words and Music by Avril Lavigne and Lukasz Gottwald

CD2 4

Intro
Moderately

Verse

1.You're not a - lone. ___ To - geth - er we stand. ___

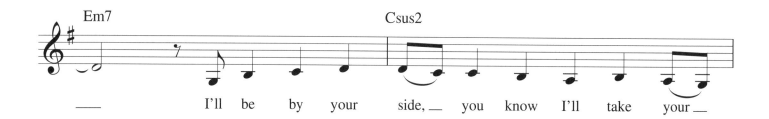

___ I'll be by your side, ___ you know I'll take your ___

hand. When it gets cold, ___ and it feels like the end, ___

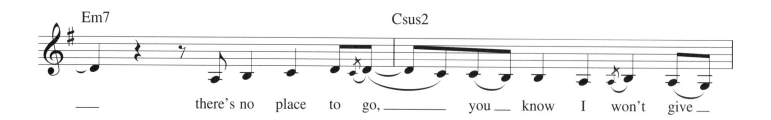

___ there's no place to go, ___ you ___ know I won't give ___

in. No, I won't give in. ___

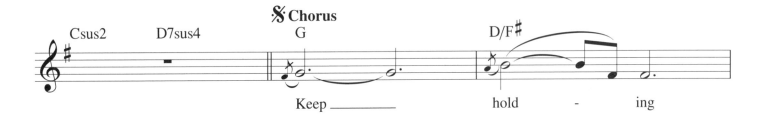

%Chorus

Csus2 D7sus4 G D/F#

Keep _____ hold - ing

Em7 Csus2

on, _____ 'cause you know we'll make it through, we'll make it through.

G D/F#

Just _____ stay _____

Em7 Csus2

strong, ____ 'cause you know I'm here for you, I'm here for you.

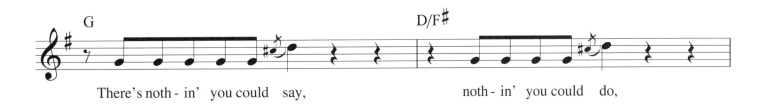

G D/F#

There's noth - in' you could say,   noth - in' you could do,

Em7 Csus2

there's no oth - er way when it comes _____ to the truth. _____ So

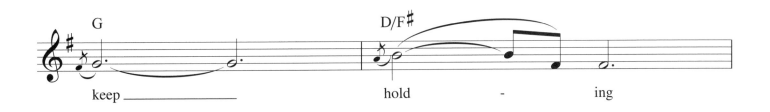

G D/F#

keep _____ hold - ing

81

on, _____ 'cause you know we'll make it through, we'll make it through.

Verse

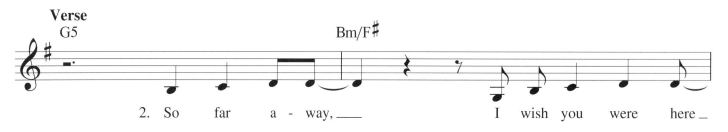

2. So far a - way, ___ I wish you were here _

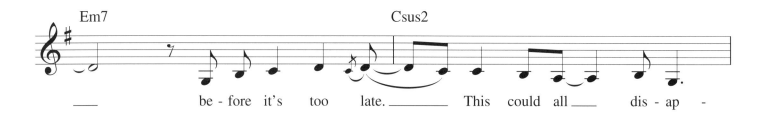

___ be - fore it's too late. _____ This could all ___ dis - ap -

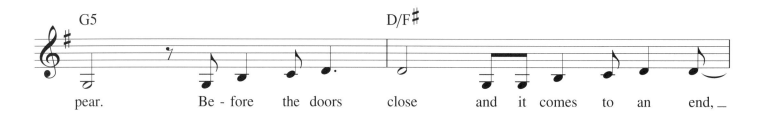

pear. Be - fore the doors close and it comes to an end, _

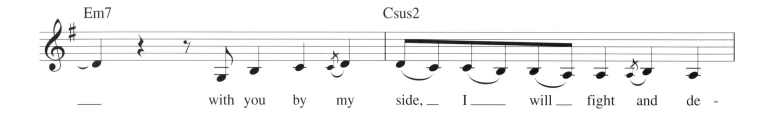

___ with you by my side, _ I ___ will __ fight and de -

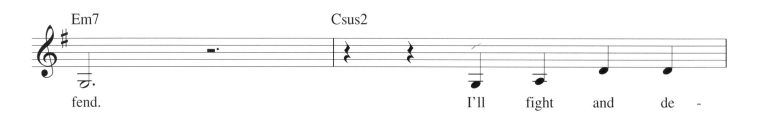

fend. I'll fight and de -

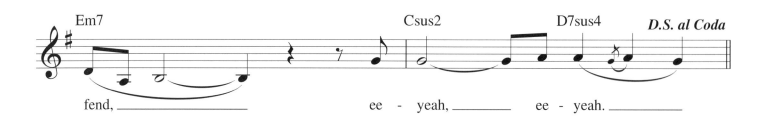

fend, _____ ee - yeah, _____ ee - yeah. ____

Coda

Bridge

Hear me when I say, when I say I be - lieve

noth - in's gon - na change, noth - in's gon - na change des - ti - ny. ____

What - ev - er's meant to be will ___ work out per - fect - ly,

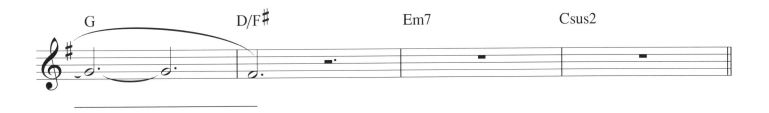

yeah, _____ yeah, _____ yeah, _____ yeah. _____

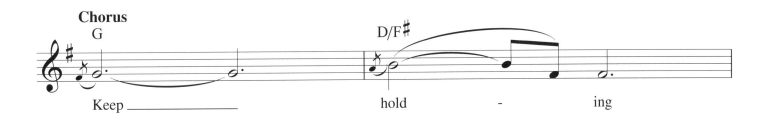

Chorus

Keep _____ hold - ing

on, ____ 'cause you know we'll make it through, we'll make it through.

Just _____ stay _____

strong, _____ 'cause you know I'm here for you, I'm here for you.

There's noth - in' you could say, noth - in' you could do,

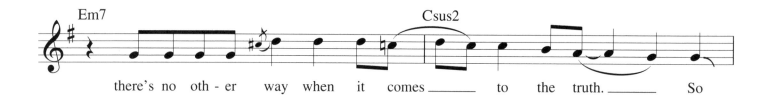

there's no oth - er way when it comes _____ to the truth. _____ So

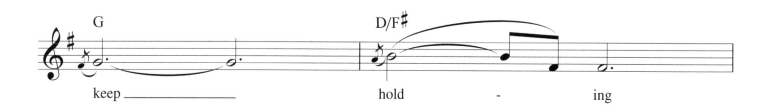

keep _____ hold - ing

on, _____ 'cause you know we'll make it through, we'll make it through.

Keep _____

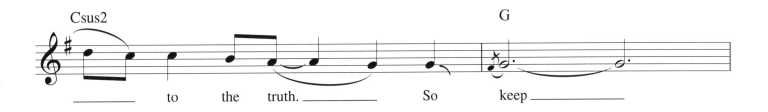

hold - ing on. _____ There's noth - in' you could   say,

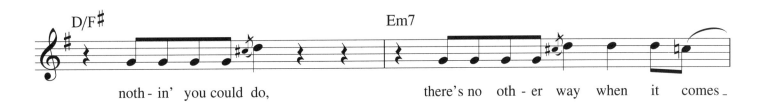

noth - in' you could do,   there's no oth - er way when it comes _

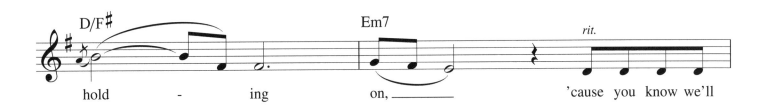

_____ to the truth. _____ So keep _____

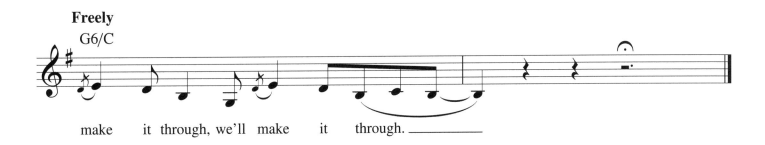

hold - ing on, _____ 'cause you know we'll

Freely

make it through, we'll make it through. _____

Killing Me Softly with His Song

Words by Norman Gimbel
Music by Charles Fox

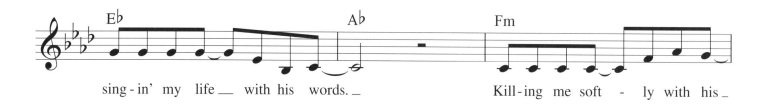

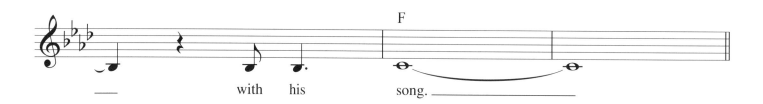

87

with his song.

Verse

B♭m7   E♭9   A♭

2. I felt all flushed _ with fe - ver, _____ em - bar - rassed _

D♭maj7   B♭m7   E♭7

_ by the _ crowd. _____ I felt he found _ my let - ters and

Fm   B♭m7

read each _ one out _ loud. _____ I prayed _ that he _

E♭7   A♭   C7

_ would fin - ish, but he just kept _ right on. _____

Chorus

Fm   B♭m7

Strum - min' my pain _ with his fin - gers, _____

E♭7   A♭   Fm

sing - in' my life _ with his words. _ Kill - ing me soft - ly with his _

B♭7/D   E♭   D♭

_ song, kill - ing me soft - ly _____ with his _ song, tell - in' my whole _

To Coda ⊕

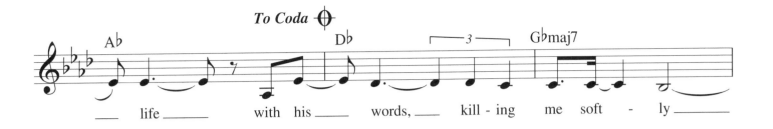

life _____ with his _____ words, ____ kill - ing me soft - ly ____

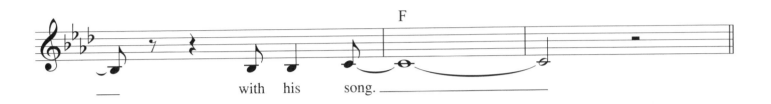

___ with his song. _____

Verse

3. He sang as if ____ he knew _ me _____ in ___ all ___ my _

___ dark _ de - spair, _____ and then he looked _ right through _ me as

if I ____ was - n't there. ___ And he ___ just kept _

D.S. al Coda

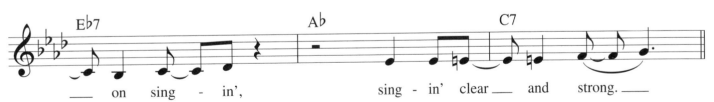

___ on sing - in', sing - in' clear ___ and strong. ___

⊕ **Coda**

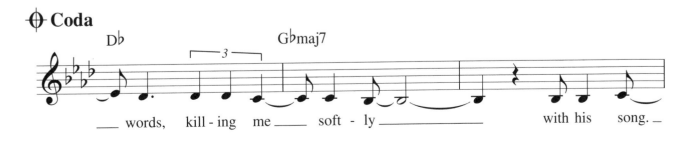

___ words, kill - ing me ___ soft - ly _____ with his song. _

89

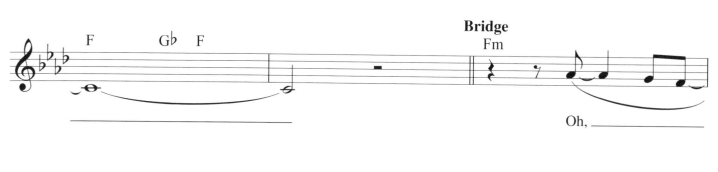

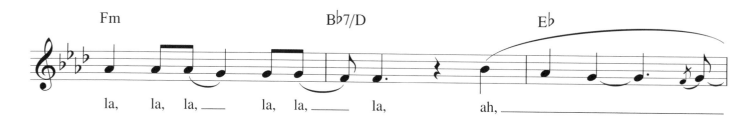

la, la, la, ___ la, la, ___ la, ___ ah, ___

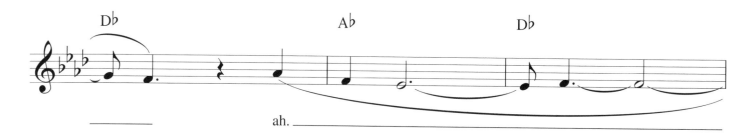

ah. ___

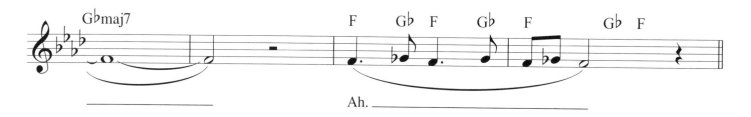

Ah. ___

Chorus

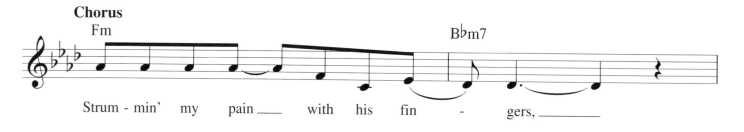

Strum - min' my pain ___ with his fin - gers, ___

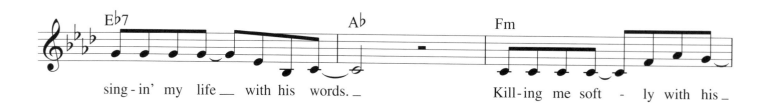

sing - in' my life ___ with his words. ___ Kill - ing me soft - ly with his ___

90

_ song, kill - ing _ me soft - ly _ with his _ song, tell - in' my _

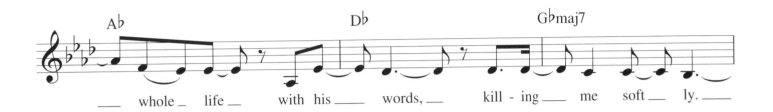

_ whole _ life _ with his _ words, _ kill - ing _ me soft _ ly. _

Outro-Chorus

He was strum - min' my pain, _

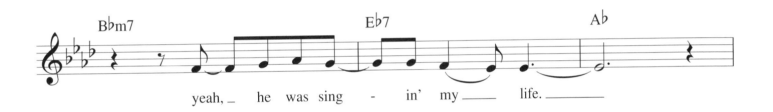

yeah, _ he was sing - in' my _ life. _

Kill-ing me soft - ly with his _ song, kill - ing me soft - ly _ with his _

_ song, tell - in' my whole _ life _ with his _ words, kill - ing _ me _

_ soft - ly _ with his song. _

Material Girl

Words by Peter Brown and Robert Rans

CD2 05

Intro
Moderately

Play 4 times

Verse

1. Some boys kiss _ me, some _ boys hug _ me. I _____ think they're O. K. _
3. *See additional lyrics*

_____ If they don't give _ me prop - er cred - it I _

_____ just walk _ a - way. _____

2. They can beg _ and they _
4., 5. *See additional lyrics*

_____ can plead _ but they _____ can't see the light. _____ (That's right.)

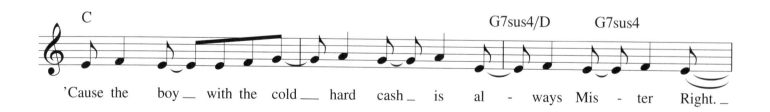

'Cause the boy _ with the cold _ hard cash _ is al - ways Mis - ter Right. _

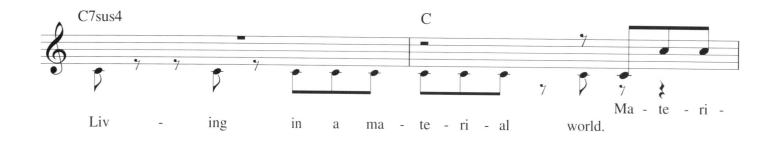

C7sus4   C

Liv - ing   in   a   ma - te - ri - al   world.   Ma - te - ri -

D.S. al Coda

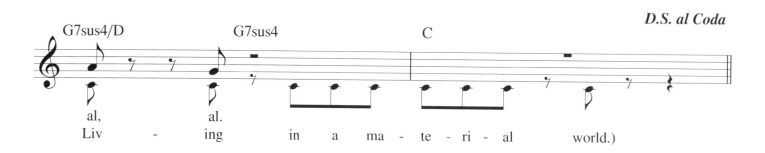

G7sus4/D   G7sus4   C

al,   al.
Liv - ing   in   a   ma - te - ri - al   world.)

Coda

F   G   Am

Liv - ing   in   a   ma - te - ri - al   world __   and   I __

F   G   Am   G

__ am   a   ma - te - ri - al   girl. __   You   know __   that   we   are

F   G   Am

liv - ing   in   a   ma - te - ri - al   world __   and   I __

F   G   C7sus4

__ am   a   ma - te - ri - al   girl. __

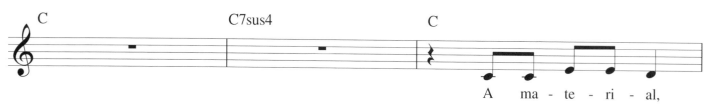

C   C7sus4   C

A   ma - te - ri - al,

a ma - te - ri - al,   a ma - te - ri - al,   a ma - te - ri - al

Outro

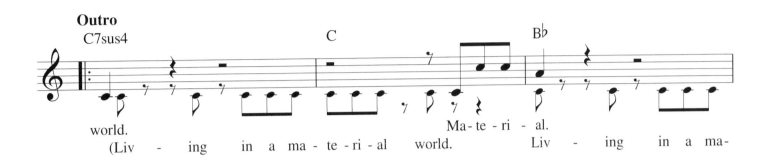

world.
(Liv - ing in a ma - te - ri - al world.   Ma - te - ri - al.   Liv - ing in a ma-

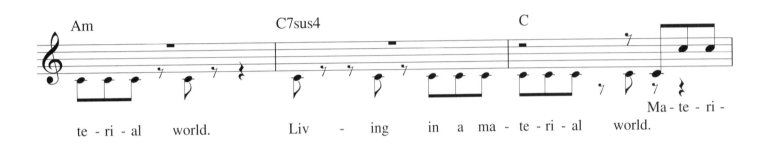

te - ri - al world.   Liv - ing in a ma - te - ri - al world.   Ma - te - ri -

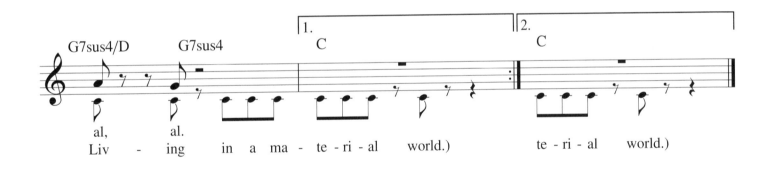

al,   al.
Liv - ing in a ma - te - ri - al world.)   te - ri - al world.)

Additional Lyrics

3. Some boys romance, some boys slow dance.
   That's all right with me.
   If they can't raise my int'rest
   Then I have to let them be.

4. Some boys try and some boys lie
   But I don't let them play.
   Only boys who save their pennies
   Make my rainy day.

5. Boys may come and boys may go and
   That's all right, you see.
   Experience has made me rich
   And now they're after me.
   'Cause ev'rybody's living...

Me and Bobby McGee

Words and Music by Kris Kristofferson and Fred Foster

Intro
Moderately

Verse

1. Bust-ed flat___ in Bat-on Rouge,

wait-in'___ for a ___ train.___ And I's feel-in' near as fad-ed as ___ my ___

jeans. ___ Bob-by thumbed ___ a die-sel down ___

just be-fore ___ it rained. ___ He rode us all the way to New Or -

leans. ___ Well I pulled my har-poon ___ out of ___ my ___

dirt-y red ___ ban-dan-na. And I's play-in' soft ___ while Bob-by sang the blues. ___

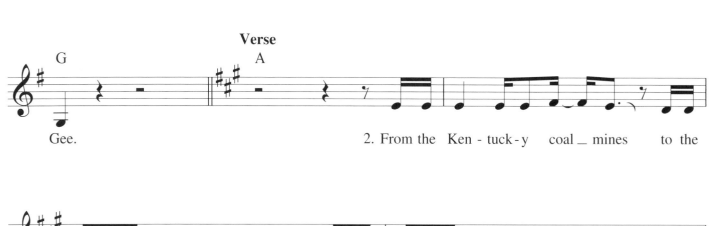

Gee.   2. From the Ken - tuck - y   coal _ mines   to the

Cal - i - for - nia sun, _   Yeah, Bob - by shared _ the se - crets of _ my _

_ soul.   And through all _   kind _ of weath - er, _   through

ev - 'ry - thing _ we done, _   yeah Bob-by, ba - by help _ me from _ this cold _

_ world. _   A one   day   up   near Sa - lin - as, Lord, _

I let him _ slip a - way. _   He's _ look - in' for that home, _ and I hope he

finds _ it. _   But I'd trade all my to - mor - rows _ for one

na, na, na, __ na, na. __ La, na, na, na, na, __ na, Bob - by __

E

__ Mc - Gee, __ yeah. __ La, nay, na, __ na, na, __ na.

La, nay, na, __ na, na. __ La, nay, na, __ na, na, __ na, Bob - by __

A

__ Mc - Gee, __ yeah. __ La, na, na. La, nay, nay, no, __ nay, nay, no, __ nay, now.

La, nay, nay, no, __ nay, nay, no, __ nay, no. Hey, now Bob - by say now Bob-by Mc-Gee, _

E7

____ yeah. __ La, nay, nay, no, __ nay, nay, no, __ nay, now. La, nay, nay, no, _

__ nay, nay, no, __ nay, nay, no, __ nay, nay, no, __ nay, now.

Hey now, Bob - by say now Bob - by Mc - Gee,

_____ yeah. _ Well, _ I called _ him my lov - er, I called him my man, ___ and I

called him my lov - er just the best I ___ can. ___ Come on, ___

and it's Bob - by now, ___ it's Bob - by Mc - Gee, ___

___ yeah. _ La, _ nay, na, ___ nay, na, ___ nay, na, ___ nay, na, ___ nay, na, ___

___ nay, na, ___ nay, na, ___ ah. ___ Hey, hey, hey, Bob - by Mc - Gee. ___

Woo.

Midnight Train to Georgia

Words and Music by Jim Weatherly

Intro
Moderately slow

1. Mm, _

Verse

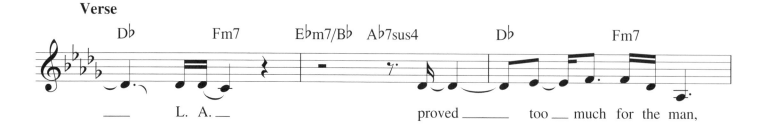

__ L. A. __ proved _____ too _ much for the man,

so he's leav-in' the life, mm, he's _

__ come to know. __ Oo, __ hoo, __ hoo.

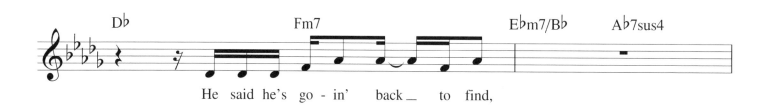

He said he's go-in' back _ to find,

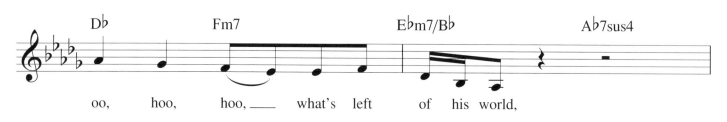

oo, hoo, hoo, __ what's left of his world,

Verse

2. He ___ kept dream - in', oo, ___ that some -
day ___ he'd be a star.
But he sure found out the hard ___ way that dreams ___ don't ___ al -
- ways come ___ true. Oh, no. Ah, ah. So he ___
___ pawned all his hopes ___ and he e -
ven sold ___ his old car, mm. Bought a
one - way tick - et back ___ to the life ___ he ___

The Way We Were

from the Motion Picture THE WAY WE WERE

Words by Alan and Marilyn Bergman
Music by Marvin Hamlisch

CD2-14

we _ left be - hind, _____ smiles we gave to one an - oth - er _____

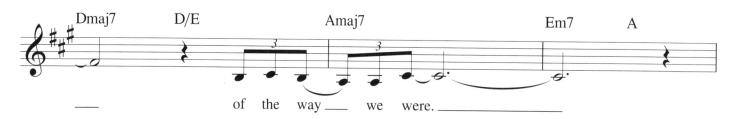

_____ of the way _____ we were. _____

Bridge

Can it be _____ that it was all _____ so sim - ple then,

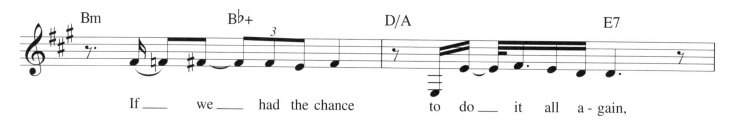

or has time _____ re - writ - ten ev - 'ry _____ line? _____

If _____ we _____ had the chance to do _____ it all a - gain,

Verse

tell me, would we? Could we? _____ 3. Mem - 'ries _____

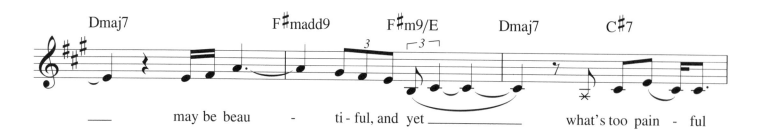

_____ may be beau - ti - ful, and yet _____ what's too pain - ful

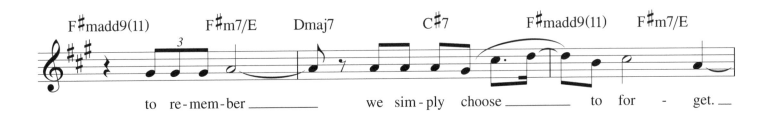

to re-mem-ber _____ we sim-ply choose _____ to for - get. _____

_____ So _____ it's _ the laugh - ter _____ we _____ will _____

_____ re - mem - ber. _____ When - ev - er we _____ re - mem - ber _____

Outro

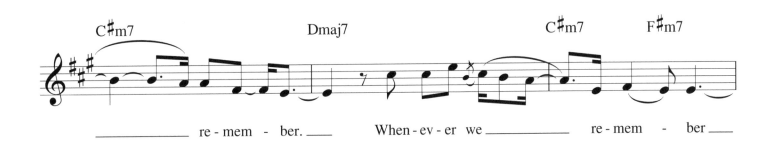

___ the way we were. _____ The way ___ we

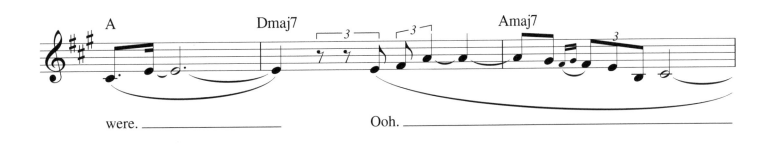

were. _____ Ooh. _____

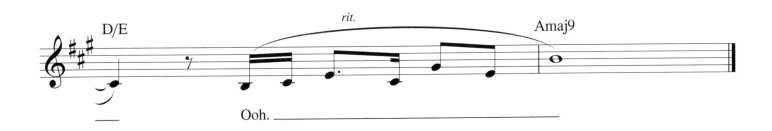

___ Ooh. _____

My Heart Will Go On
(Love Theme from 'Titanic')

from the Paramount and Twentieth Century Fox Motion Picture

Music by James Horner
Lyric by Will Jennings

CD2 08

Intro

Verse

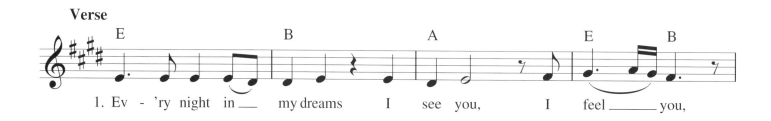

1. Ev - 'ry night in __ my dreams I see you, I feel ____ you,

that is how I __ know you go __ on. ____

Far a-cross the __ dis-tance and spac-es __ be - tween ___ us

you have come to __ show you go on. ____

Chorus

Near, far, wher-ev - er __ you are, __ I be -

lieve ___ that the heart does go on. _____

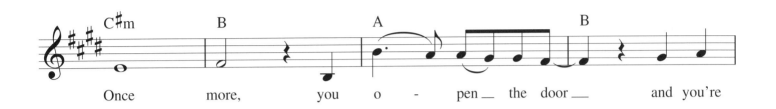

Once more, you o - pen ___ the door ___ and you're

here ___ in ___ my ___ heart, and my heart will go on ___ and ___ on.

Verse

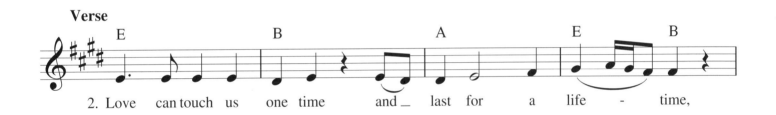

2. Love can touch us one time and ___ last for a life - time,

and nev - er let ___ go till we're gone.

Love was when I ___ loved you, one ___ true time I hold _____ to.

In my life we'll al - ways go _____ on. _____

111

Chorus

Near, far, wher - ev - er you are, I be -

lieve that the heart does go on.

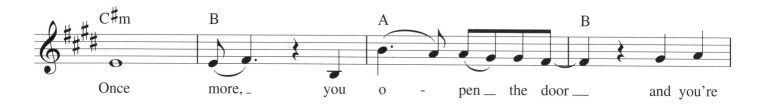

Once more, you o - pen the door and you're

here in my heart, and my heart will go on and

Interlude

on.

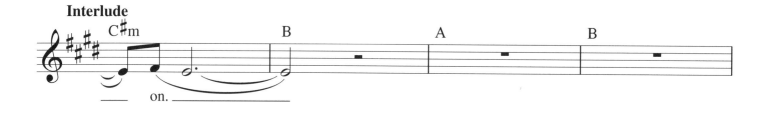

Chorus

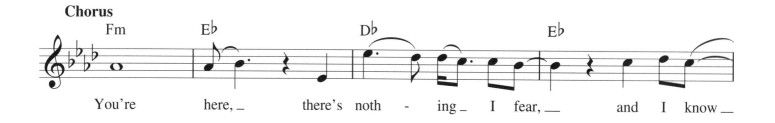

You're here, there's noth - ing I fear, and I know

My Life Would Suck Without You

Words and Music by Lukasz Gottwald, Max Martin and Claude Kelly

Intro
Moderately

Verse

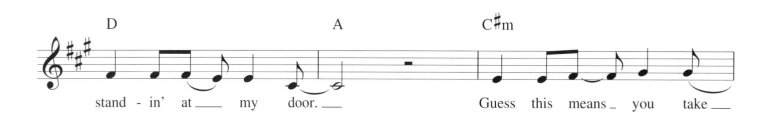

Guess this means _ you're sor - ry, you're

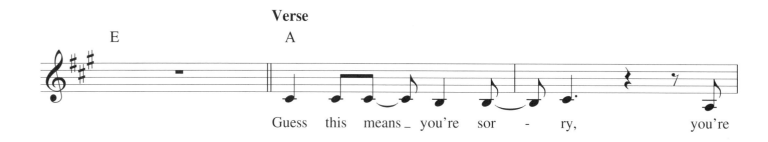

stand - in' at _ my door. _ Guess this means _ you take _

_ back _ all you said _ be - fore. _

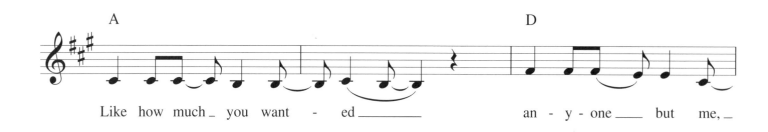

Like how much _ you want - ed _____ an - y-one ___ but me, _

said you'd nev - er come __ back, __ but

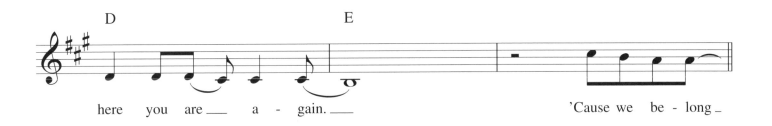

here you are __ a - gain. __ 'Cause we be - long __

𝄋 Chorus

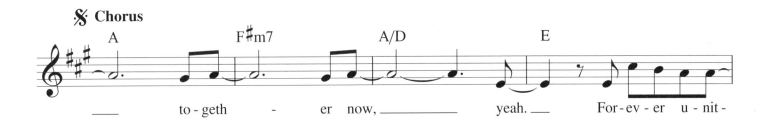

__ to - geth - er now, _____ yeah. __ For - ev - er u - nit -

- ed here __ some - how, _____ yeah. __ You got a piece __

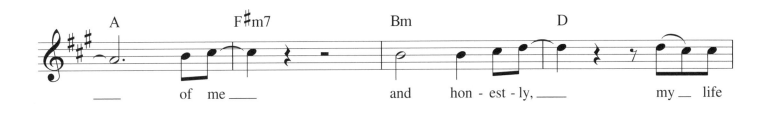

__ of me __ and hon - est - ly, _____ my __ life

To Coda ⊕ **Verse**

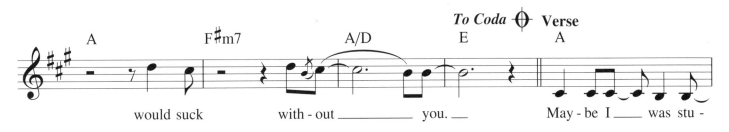

would suck with - out _____ you. __ May - be I __ was stu -

- pid   for   tell - in' you __ good - bye. __   May - be I __ was   wrong __

__ for __   try-in' to pick __ a   fight. __   I   know that I've __ got   is -

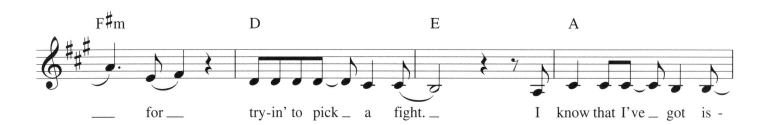

- sues,   but you're pret - ty   messed __ up, too. __   Ei - ther way __ I   found __

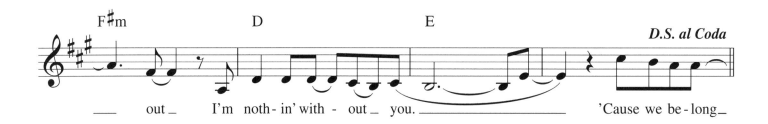

__ out __   I'm noth- in' with - out __ you. _____   'Cause we be - long __

Verse
Coda

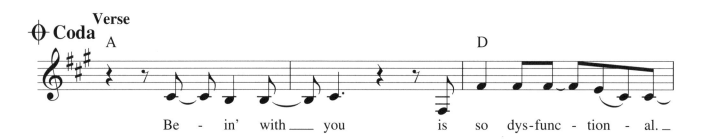

Be - in'   with __ you   is   so   dys-func - tion - al. __

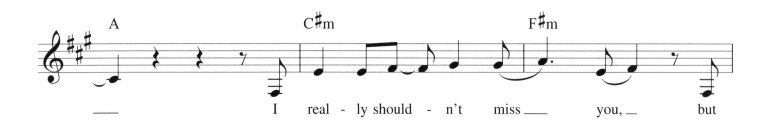

__   I   real - ly should - n't   miss ___   you, __   but

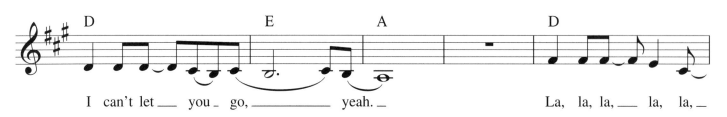

I   can't let __ you _ go, _____   yeah. __   La, la, la, __ la, la,

116

la, la, la, __ la, la, __ la. __ La, la, la, __ la, la. __

Chorus-Outro

'Cause we be-long __ to-geth - er now, __

__ yeah. __ For-ev-er u - nit - ed here __ some-how, __

__ yeah. __ You got a piece __ of me __

and hon-est-ly, __ my __ life would suck with-out __

__ you. __ 'Cause we be-long __ __

Poker Face

Words and Music by Stefani Germanotta and RedOne

Intro
Moderately

Verse

I wan - na hold 'em like they do in Tex - as, please.

Fold 'em, let 'em hit me, raise it. Ba - by, stay with me.

Luck and in - tu - i - tion play the cards with spades to start. And

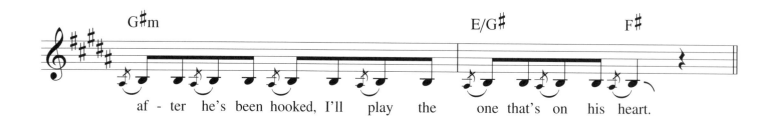

af - ter he's been hooked, I'll play the one that's on his heart.

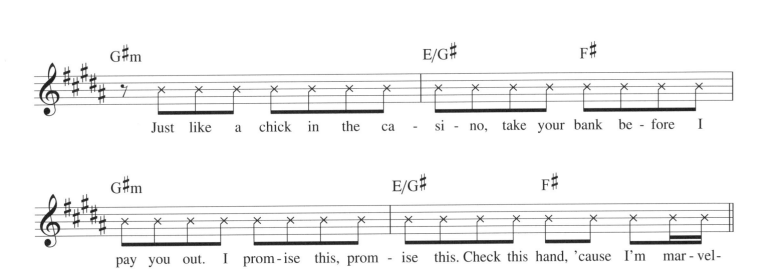

Just like a chick in the ca - si - no, take your bank be - fore I

pay you out. I prom - ise this, prom - ise this. Check this hand, 'cause I'm mar - vel -

Chorus

ous. Can't read my, ___ can't read my, ___ no, he can't read - a my

pok - er face. ___

Can't read my, ___ can't read my, ___ no, he can't read - a my

Sing 3 times

pok - er face. ___

Outro

P - p - p - pok - er face, p - p - pok - er face. ___

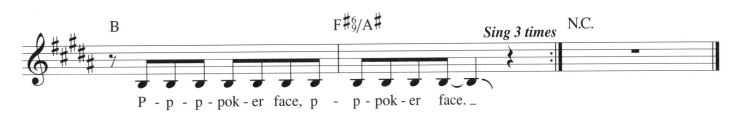

Sing 3 times N.C.

P - p - p - pok - er face, p - p - pok - er face. ___

The Power of Love

Words by Mary Susan Applegate and Jennifer Rush
Music by Candy Derouge and Gunther Mende

Slowly

Verse

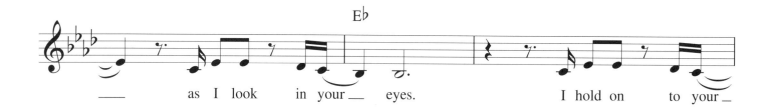

1. The whis-pers ___ in the morn-ing ___ of lov-ers sleep-

-ing ___ tight ___ are roll-ing by ___ like thun-der now ___

___ as I look in your ___ eyes. I hold on to your ___

___ bod-y ___ and feel each ___ move ___ you ___ make. ___

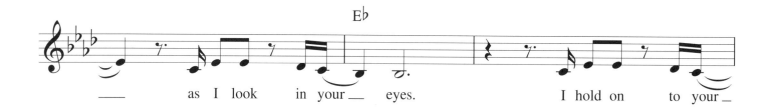

___ Your voice is warm and ___ ten-der, ___ a love that I could not for-

Chorus

-sake. ___ 'Cause I'm your la-dy, ___

Outro-Chorus

Begin fade

Fade out

Rehab

Words and Music by Amy Winehouse

They tried to make me go to re - hab, ___ I ___ said,

"no, ___ no, ___ no." Yes, ___ I been ___ black, but when ___

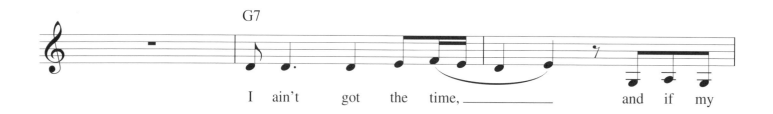

___ I come ___ back you'll ___ know, ___ know, ___ know.

I ain't got the time, ___ and if my

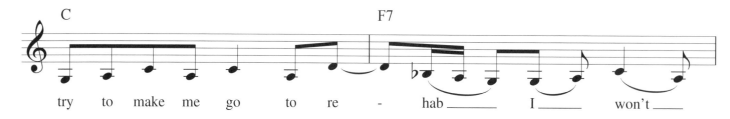

dad - dy ___ thinks ___ I'm fine, ___ just

try to make me go to re - hab ___ I ___ won't ___

Verse

1. I'd rath - er be _____ at home _____ _____ with Ray. I ain't got _____ _____ sev - en - teen days. _____ 'Cause there's noth - in', _____ there's noth - in' you _____ can _____ teach me that I can't learn _____ from Mis - ter Hath - a - way. _____ I did - n't

get a lot in class, _____

F7
but I know ___ it ___ don't come

D.S. al Coda
in ___ a ___ shot glass. They

⊕ Coda
Verse
Em
2. The man said, "Why do you think you ___

Am
___ here?" ___ I said,

A♭7
"I got no ___ i - dea. ___

Em
I'm gon - na, I'm

Am
gon - na lose ___ my ___ ba - by, ___

Verse

Em

3. I don't ev - er wan - na drink _____

Am   F7

_____ a - gain.   I just,

Ab7

ooh, _____ just _____ need _____ a friend. _____

Em

_____ I'm not _____ gon - na spend _____ ten _____

Am   F7

_____ weeks, _   have ev - 'ry - one

Ab7

think   I'm   on _____ the _____ mend. _____

G7

It's   not   just   my   pride, _____

F7

It's   just _____ 'til   these

tears   have _____   dried. _____   They

Chorus

C7

Tried to make me go to re - hab, _____ I _____ said, _____

"No, _____   no, _____   no."   Yes, ___

___ I've been ___ black, but when ___ I come ___ back, you'll ___

G7

know, _____ know, ___ know.   I ain't got the time, ___

F7

_____   and if my dad - dy _____ thinks ___ I'm fine, ___

C

just try to make me go to re -

F7   C

- hab, _____ I _____ won't _____ go, _____ go, _____ go.

131

Total Eclipse of the Heart

Words and Music by Jim Steinman

___us. Ev-'ry now and then I get a lit-tle bit ter - ri-fied and then I see the look in your eyes. _

Pre-Chorus

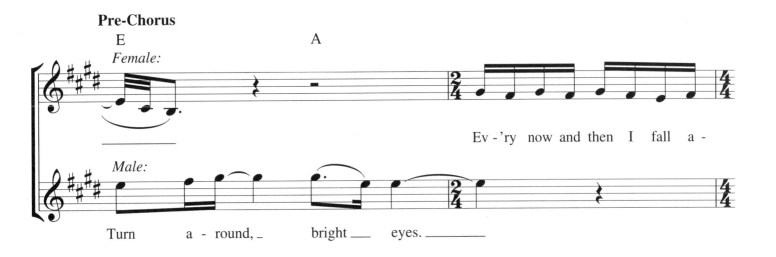

_____   Ev -'ry now and then I fall a -

Turn   a - round, _   bright ___ eyes. _____

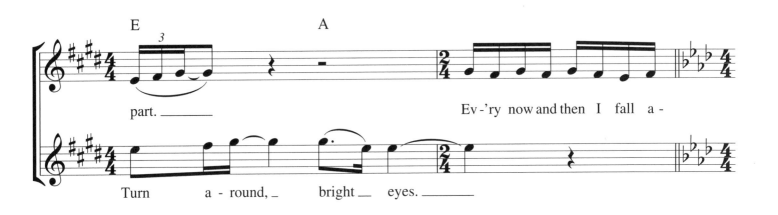

part. _____   Ev -'ry now and then I fall a -

Turn   a - round, _   bright ___ eyes. _____

Chorus

part.   And I need you now _ to - night, _   and I need you more _____ than

ev - er.   And if you on - ly hold _ me tight, _   we'll be hold - in' on _ for -

Ab   Fm7   Db   Eb7

ev - er. And we'll on - ly be mak - in' it right _ 'cause we'll nev-er be wrong. _ To-

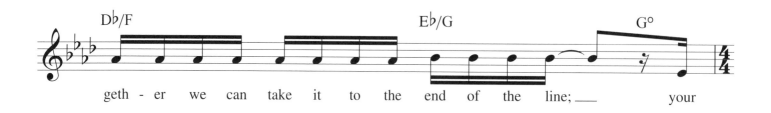

Db/F   Eb/G   G°

geth - er we can take it to the end of the line; ___ your

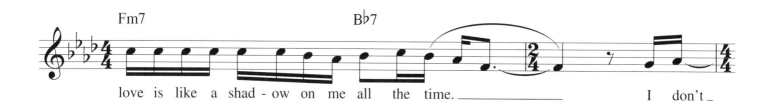

Fm7   Bb7

love is like a shad - ow on me all the time. _____ I don't _

Ab   Eb/G

___ know what to do, ___ I'm al - ways in the dark. ___ We're

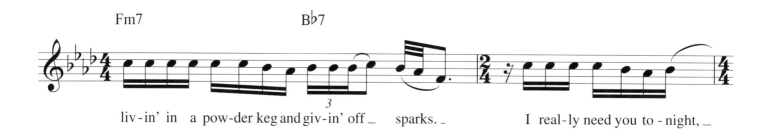

Fm7   Bb7

liv - in' in a pow - der keg and giv - in' off _ sparks. _ I real - ly need you to - night, _

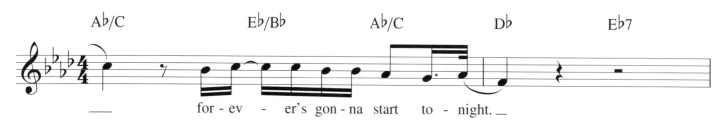

Ab/C   Eb/Bb   Ab/C   Db   Eb7

___ for - ev - er's gon - na start to - night. _

Once up-on a time, I was fall-ing in love, ___ now I'm on-ly fall-ing a - part. ___

___ There's noth-in' I can do, a to-tal e - clipse ___ of the heart. ___

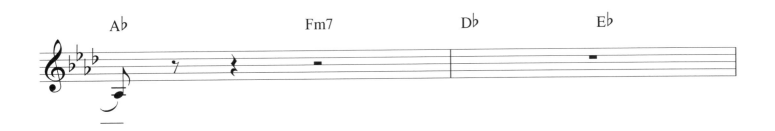

Female:

Once up-on a time, there was light in my life, ___ now there's on-ly love in the dark. ___

Male:

Now there's on-ly love in the dark. ___

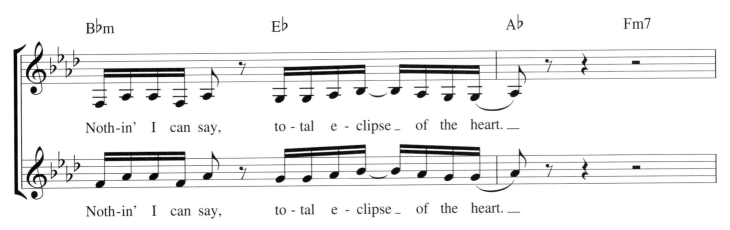

Noth-in' I can say, to-tal e - clipse ___ of the heart. ___

Noth-in' I can say, to-tal e - clipse ___ of the heart. ___

Interlude

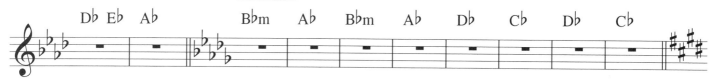

Pre-Chorus

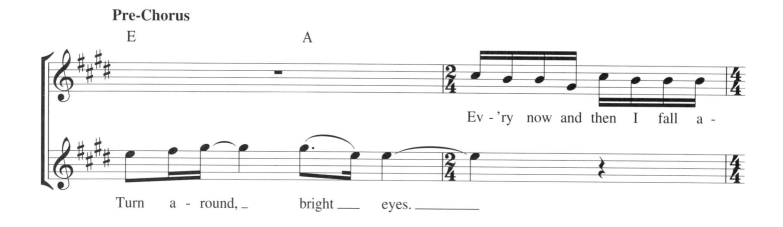

Ev - 'ry now and then I fall a-

Turn a - round, __ bright __ eyes. _____

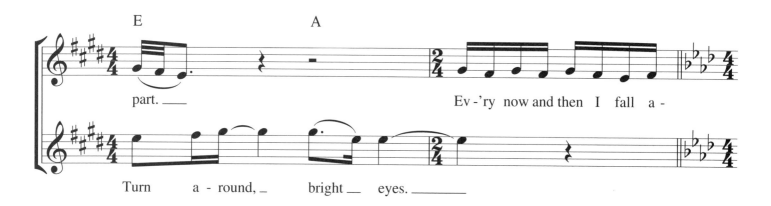

part. ____

Ev - 'ry now and then I fall a-

Turn a - round, __ bright __ eyes. _____

Chorus

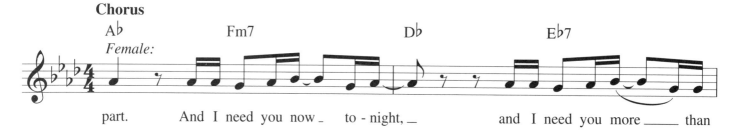

part.   And I need you now _ to - night, _   and I need you more _____ than

ev - er.   And if you'll on - ly hold _ me tight, ___   we'll be hold - in' on _____ for-

ev - er.   And we'll on - ly be mak - in' it right _   'cause we'll nev - er be wrong. __ To-

136

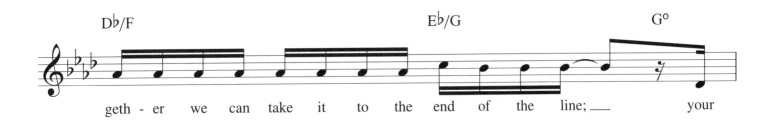

geth - er we can take it to the end of the line; ___ your

love is like a shad-ow on me all of the time. _____ I don't ___

___ know what to do, ___ I'm al - ways in the dark. ___ We're

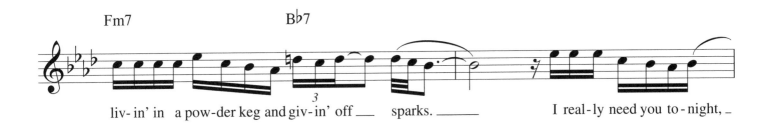

liv-in' in a pow-der keg and giv-in' off ___ sparks. _____ I real-ly need you to - night, __

___ for - ev - er's gon-na start __ to - night. ____

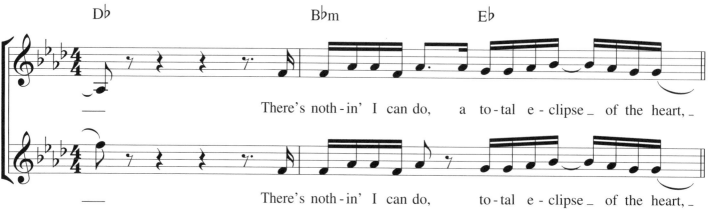

Outro

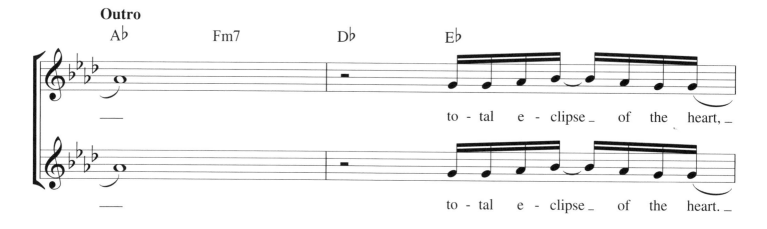

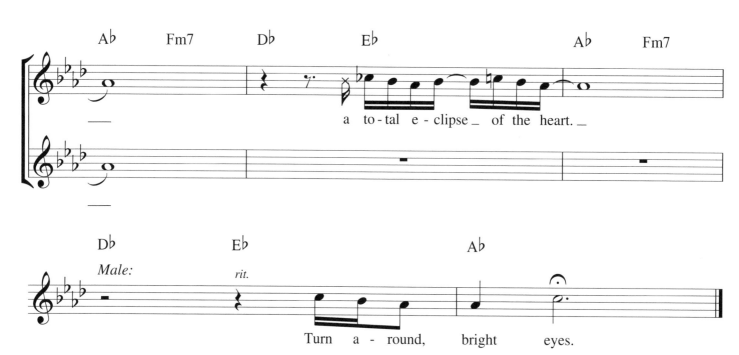

Who Knew

Words and Music by Alecia Moore, Max Martin and Lukasz Gottwald

CD 2 15

Verse

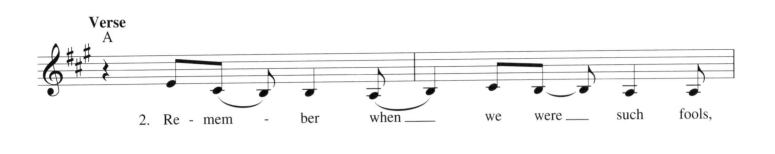

2. Re - mem - ber when _____ we were _____ such fools,

and so _____ con - vinced, _____ and just _____ too _____ cool? _____

Bm   F#m   E5

_____ Oh   no, _____   no,   no. _____

A

I   wish _____ I   could _____ touch you _____ a - gain.

I   wish _____ I   could _____ still   call _____ you   a   friend, _____

Bm7   F#m   E5

_____ I'd   give _____   an - y - thing.

Chorus

Dsus2   E

When   some - one _____ said, "Count your bless - ings   now, _____

Un - til ___ we, un - til ___ we meet ___ a - gain. ___

Bm   **F#m**   **E**

I won't ___ for - get ___ you, my ___ friend, what hap - pened?

Chorus

Dsus2   **E**

If some - one ___ said three years ___ from now ___

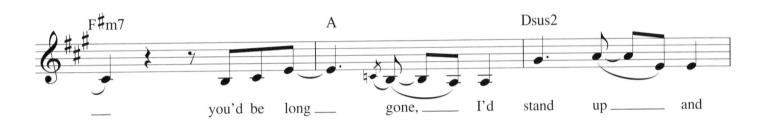

F#m7   **A**   **Dsus2**

___ you'd be long ___ gone, ___ I'd stand up ___ and

E   **F#m7**   **A**

punch them ___ out, ___ 'cause they're all ___ wrong, _ and

Dsus2   **E**   **F#m7**

our last ___ kiss ___ I'll cher - ish un - til ___ we meet _

A   **Dsus2**   **E**

___ a - gain. ___ And time _ makes _ it hard - er.

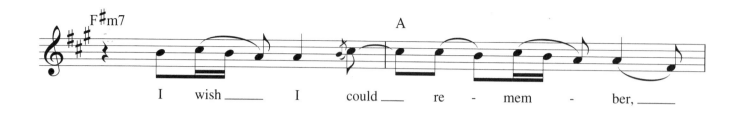

I wish ____ I could ____ re - mem - ber, ____

but I ____ keep ____ your mem - 'ry. You vis - it me ____

____ in ____ my ____ sleep. ____ My dar - lin', ____ who ____ knew?

Outro

My dar - lin', my dar - lin',

who ____ knew? My dar - lin', I miss ____ you.

my dar - lin', who ____ knew?